THE
30-MINUTE
DECORATOR

Front cover photographs:
(left) Robert Harding Syndication/Ideal Home/Di Lewis;
(centre right) Eaglemoss Publications/Graham Rae; (bottom right) Rubber Stampede Co.
Back cover: (top left) Eaglemoss Publications/Graham Rae;
(top right, bottom) Eaglemoss Publications/Lizzie Orme.

Photographs page 1 Ariadne, Holland, 3 Marie Claire Idées/Gaillard/Chastres/Chombart,
4 Eaglemoss/Graham Rae, 5(tr) Robert Harding Syndication/Homes and Gardens/David Barrett, (br)
Eaglemoss/Adrian Taylor, 6 Eaglemoss/Lizzie Orme.

First published in North America
in 1998 by Betterway Books
an imprint of F&W Publications, Inc.
1507 Dana Avenue
Cincinnati, Ohio 45207
1-800-289-0963

ISBN 1-55870-498-1

Printed in China

10 9 8 7 6

THE
30-MINUTE
DECORATOR

BETTERWAY BOOKS
Cincinnati, Ohio

CONTENTS

QUICK PAINTING PROJECTS

FABRIC FIX-UPS

DECORATING WITH FOUND OBJECTS

Style on Display

Instant Flower Arrangements

Little Luxuries

STENCILLING

Stencilled designs add originality and charm to plain surfaces. Use them to give a fresh look to furniture, accessories and walls.

Stencilling is a quick, easy and rewarding paint technique that, with a little practice, gives a crisp, clean motif every time. Stencils can be used to decorate almost any surface. You just need to choose the appropriate type of paint for the surface. A huge range of pre-cut stencil designs is available from craft shops, department stores and by mail order.

There are several ways you can apply the paint to the stencil – using a foam paint roller or sponge applicator, a stiff-bristled stencil brush or spray paint.

Oil, acrylic and special stencil paints, crayons and cremes are all suitable for stencilling on wood and walls. The paint must be the right consistency: if it is too thin it will run; too thick and it will clog the stencil. Practise stencilling on a sheet of paper before working on the item itself, but don't worry if you make mistakes – the charm of stencilling is its handcrafted look.

▲ *This pea flower motif gives a charming country cottage feel to this kitchen. For a coordinated look, use the whole design on a conspicuous feature, such as a kitchen cupboard, and stencil parts of the motif on walls, furniture and accessories.*

You can adapt your stencil design to suit the size and shape of the item you are decorating. Here the pea pods are used on the top of a small stool, while the flowers, leaves and tendrils trail along its sides. The floral section of the stencil fits neatly on the sides of the planter.

A trail of three pink pea flowers stencilled directly above an iron peg rail softens its stark lines, and is perfectly in keeping with the peg rail's rustic air.

Give a wooden trug a facelift with a wash of paint and stencilled pea flowers in pale yellow.

STENCILLING CHAIRBACKS

Stencil a pretty design on to a plain kitchen chair to recapture the look of traditional country kitchen furniture. Sponge on the stencil design for a soft look using the colours of your kitchen.

▼ *This simple iris stencil looks really pretty on the back rest of a natural beech chair, but it would work just as well on a painted chair.*

◄ *Ladder-back chairs like these are perfect for stencilling. You can paint them with the same design, as on the chairbacks, or choose a different design for each one, as on the chair fronts. Here, the top of each slat is painted bright red for a jolly splash of colour.*

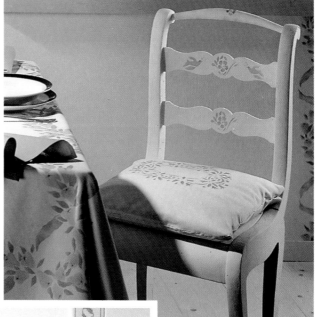

▲ *This chair has been stencilled with pretty flower and dove motifs to co-ordinate with the stencilled cushion. The full design is used on the top slat, with just the floral motif on the lower slat.*

◄ *Chairs with solid backs are also perfect for stencilling. You could use the whole motif along the top, with the centre motif arranged at angles over the rest of the back. To vary the effect even more, you could enlarge the centre design on a photocopier to make a larger stencil.*

STENCILLING WITH SPRAY PAINTS

*Spray paints make light work of stencilling projects.
They're easy to apply, quick-drying and won't seep under
the stencil to form smudges.*

As well as giving you instant, effortless results, stencilling using spray paints allows you to create a number of different effects. You can apply several light coats of paint to build up solid colour and a clearly outlined design; spray a fine mist over the stencil to give a soft, hazy finish; or layer up different spray paint colours to create exciting mottled and shaded effects which will give your design a sense of depth.

The following page shows two spray stencilling techniques – one using an ordinary acetate stencil, and the other using flat shapes, such as leaves or paper doilies, to create reversed-out or 'silhouette' stencilled designs.

Enamel, decorative or specially developed stencil spray

For an instant new look, this blanket box was spray painted all over, inside and out, then spray stencilled. To create clean, distinct colours, as here, spray on several light coats of each paint colour, and take care to mask off the different colour areas of the stencil as you work to prevent the paints drifting.

paints work best for stencilling. Always protect the surrounding area, and follow the manufacturer's instructions for using your particular paint.

A classic rose stencil is used large and small to decorate a range of surfaces and accessories. Although the stencil is a very simple two-colour design, the softly shaded effect created by the spray paints – especially noticeable on the lampshade – adds a new dimension.

Mottled autumnal hues and a variety of leaf shapes have been used to spray stencil this fire surround. To copy the effect, spray the surface with a base colour (yellow in this case) then position the leaves. Spray the paints on lightly and unevenly to create a patchy finish, applying and lifting off the leaves as desired between coats. Repeat on surrounding surfaces for a thoroughly themed room scheme.

Re-create the delicate tracery of fine lace on a plain tablecloth. Lay an old piece of lace – an old lace curtain is ideal – over a plain white paper or cotton tablecloth, and spray lightly over it using gold spray paint. When the paint is dry, lift off the lace. Use fabric spray paints if you are decorating a cotton cloth, and follow the paint manufacturer's instructions for washing.

FROSTING GLASS

Re-create the exquisite effect of etched or sandblasted glass using frosting varnish and stencils. You can produce any design you like, from a simple geometric border to an intricate pictorial motif.

A simple and effective way to reproduce the decorative effect of frosted glass is to brush frosting varnish on to glass over a stencil. You then give it a textured finish by stippling it with a brush or running a paint roller over it.

Using stencils means you can create as simple or intricate a design as you like – dainty flowers or butterflies, for example, on a glass vase or bottle, a geometric border around the edges of a window pane, or a finely detailed floral design swirling down the centre of a glass cupboard door.

As with any stencilling project, it's easiest to work on a flat surface, so avoid curved glass items such as round vases. If you make a mistake or decide you don't like the finished effect, you can remove the frosting varnish using methylated spirits/ denatured alcohol.

Clean the glass with soapy water before stencilling. Once the stencilling has been successfully applied, clean

Add character to the glass doors of a kitchen cupboard with a stencilled frosted motif. Here a floral motif is worked in mirror image, first on the top half of the door, then on the bottom half. Work the stencil on the inside of the glass to protect it.

the frosted glass with warm soapy water and wipe over it gently; do not use solvent-based window cleaning agents.

The frosted sun motif on this lantern is thrown into relief by the bright candle flame behind it. Try to choose a stencil design that is in keeping with the item you're decorating – stars and crescent moons would also be appropriate choices for a lantern.

Update an old glass-topped table with an elegant frosted design. Here, an ivy wreath motif adds detailing to this glass table top. A coloured tablecloth placed under the glass subtly alters the colouring and texture of the frosted design.

Bottles of bath oil are given an exquisite finish with delicate frosted bee and bow motifs, which stand out well against their coloured backgrounds.

TILE EFFECTS

*Give your old kitchen or bathroom tiles a modern,
up-to-the-minute look with a range of decorative paint
techniques. Or apply stick-on motifs to plain tiles.*

Removing old tiles can be a costly and rather messy operation. So if you're bored with your existing tiles, or have moved and want to redecorate but can't afford to replace the tiles, don't despair. There's a number of easy options you can use to brighten up old tiles – applying a handpainted design, for example, or sticking on self-adhesive or ceramic motifs. A wide range of ceramic tile motifs is available in a variety of themes.

Rag-rolling, sponging and stamping are all easy paint techniques to master and provide almost instant results on tiles. Stencilled and handpainted designs may take a little more patience to apply, but the results are well worth it.

For longlasting results when painting tiles, it's important to use the correct paint. This is essential for kitchen or bathroom tiles, which are subject to the effects of steam and condensation and require frequent cleaning. On glossy tile surfaces, acrylic enamel paints provide a fairly durable finish. But for areas which get a lot of use, it's advisable to seal the surface with ceramic varnish. Try one of the new air-dry glass and tile paints, available at craft stores. Good do-it-yourself stores also stock a number of tile cover-up products, which prime and prepare the surface ready for painting or applying stick-on motifs.

▼ ***All change*** *Liven up plain white bathroom tiles with jaunty jester crowns. Here, tiles – sectioned off with brightly painted beading at the top and decorative shelving at the lower edge – have been primed and painted in bright green. A hot glue gun makes easy work of attaching the crowns to alternate tiles.*

Transfer style Rub-on transfers give the look of handpainting or stencilling but take much less time to apply. Simply remove the protective backing, place the transfer face down on the tile and rub over the back, then gently peel away the transfer sheet.

Seeing stars Worked in different colours, a simple stamp design, applied to the ceramic tiles and floorboards in this minimalist bathroom, softens the look and creates a coordinated effect.

Kitchen medley Use stick-on ceramic motifs to add a three-dimensional look to plain tiles. These juicy vegetables are perfect for a bright, modern kitchen; or opt instead for a fruity effect. For a bathroom, look out for shell and fish motifs (see right).

Creating a buzz Cheer up a bathroom with a bee and beehive pre-cut stencil. Prime the tiles, then secure the stencil in place with masking tape before stencilling the design. For a shaded effect, use acrylic paints in two or three colours. Use the whole design to form a border and add individual bees to adjacent tiles.

STAMPED IDEAS

*Use shop-bought or home-made stamps and colourful
paints to add eye-catching detailing and a fresh
new look to room schemes and accessories.*

Stamping is an inexpensive and very quick way to decorate your home or highlight a dull corner. You can stamp on most surfaces, including painted walls, ceramic tiles, paper and fabric, and in a very short time transform the ordinary into the extraordinary. As always, the simplest and most graphic motifs are the most effective. The technique is easy to master, but it's worth practising on scrap paper first.

You can buy ready-made decorative stamps, together with stamp paints and applicators, from mail order catalogues and craft shops; or you can make your own stamps from household sponges.

The paint or ink can be applied to the stamp in a number of ways. For straightforward single colour designs, simply dip the stamp into a saucer of paint, or a paint or ink pad; alternatively, apply the paint using a small foam roller or sponge applicator.

For multi-coloured designs, colour in the different areas of the stamp using either special water-based marker pens or acrylic paints and an artists' detail brush.

Star attraction *Neat rows of stars stamped in yellow and dark blue paint outline the ceiling, skirting board and picture frames in this cheerful child's room. To give an even finish, use a piece of cardboard as a spacer and a small foam roller to apply the paint.*

On most surfaces, except fabric, any mistakes can be washed off immediately using a damp sponge.

Pleasing primitives These cushions and boxes have been stamped with a selection of primitive shapes. The stamps are sold as a themed set, so you can combine them in different ways to create a number of designs. The leaf motifs on the cushions have been quilted round for added emphasis.

Squares and stamps Stamps are ideal for transforming plain, everyday accessories into unique showpieces. This hatbox has been decorated with brightly coloured squares of paper which were stamped then glued in place. Two coats of varnish protect the finish.

Fishy finish A plain white tiled splashback has been given a fresh new look with a stamped design of fish and waves in cool green and blue. For added interest, the direction of the stamp was changed for alternate rows of tiles.

Folk art Delicate folk art patterns in several colours add charming detailing to this painted cupboard. With multi-coloured stamped motifs, each colour has to be applied to the stamp separately, so they're best used on furniture and accessories rather than large surfaces.

STAMPING DESIGNS ON FABRIC

Stamp unusual and inventive designs on fabrics, using everyday household objects – from pieces of cardboard and small blocks of wood to bottle corks and pastry cutters.

You can use almost any small object to stamp designs on fabrics. Take inspiration from the ideas shown here, and experiment with some of your own on scrap pieces of fabric or cardboard.

Use special stamp paint for the best results. It's available in a wide range of colours, including gold and silver, and is washable once fully dry. Always follow the manufacturer's instructions for a particular paint. To clean the paint off the object you're stamping with, simply rinse it in soapy water before the paint dries. Choose smooth, natural fabrics to stamp on, and wash the fabric before you begin, to pre-shrink it and to remove any manufacturer's finish.

Experiment first on a scrap of the fabric to check the effect. Tape the fabric to the work surface to prevent it from shifting during stamping. If stamping items on a double layer of fabric, as on cushion covers or shoe bags, for example, slip a sheet of plastic between the layers of fabric to prevent the paint seeping through.

Add a fun finish to children's shoe bags with some clever stamp ideas. Here, children's wellington boots have been used to stamp footprints on one bag while a train has been created using a block of wood for the carriages, a cork for the wheels and a pastry cutter for the puffs of smoke.

➤ Create a whimsical window drape by covering a length of plain voile with stamped gold stars. Simply cut a 7.5cm (3in) and a 5cm (2in) length of stiff cardboard. Dip one side edge of the longer card into gold stamp paint and stamp a horizontal then vertical line to form a cross; stamp two intersecting diagonal lines on top of this. Then use the shorter card to stamp two more diagonals over the top, to complete the star. Repeat the design at random over the fabric.

▼ Use pastry cutters and a bottle cork to create eye-catching patterns on plain cushion covers. You can repeat the motifs on other accessories in the room, for a coordinated look. Stamp with the thicker end of the pastry cutters, rather than the cutting end. Rinse the paint off the cutters straightaway using soapy water, so that you can reuse them.

▼ Plain tablelinen is a perfect candidate for creative stamping. These abstract designs are created using a triangular make-up sponge, stiff cardboard, a block of wood and a spaghetti server.

QUICK COVER-UPS

*The fashion for furniture cover-ups allows you to create
new looks, experiment with colour on a temporary basis or
quickly revive the tired image of a well-worn chair.*

Take a length of fabric, hemmed or not, toss it over a chair, catch up the corners in knots or cord and you have an instant cover-up. All kinds of fabric can be used to cover furniture, casually or artfully, disguising shabby pieces or creating an instant change of colour scheme.

Whatever piece you are covering up, you will need a generous length of fabric. This prevents the finished effect from looking skimpy, and gives you the scope to arrange the fabric to full effect. Try using a bedspread with bordered edges to cover a large armchair or sofa; or use a plain sheet, first giving it a personal touch with a stamped or stencilled design. For a smaller item, such as a side table or footstool, you could use a large shawl or simply a length of inexpensive cotton cut to size with pinking shears.

Experiment with ways to drape the fabric, using pleats and deep tucks to take up the excess and tying and knotting the corners to hold the fabric in place.

High drama *A simple dining chair lies beneath this theatrical treatment, which uses a length of exotic fabric, a few safety pins and some rubber bands. Place a generous length of fabric over the chair, tucking and pinning it into a loosely fitting shape. Twist the excess fabric into bunches at the front corners and back of the chair (right), secure with rubber bands and arrange the bunched fabric into puffy rosettes. Finish by pinking the fabric at the lower edges.*

▶ **A touch of theatre** *Covering a large item such as a sofa requires a lot of fabric. An inexpensive solution is to use a spare sheet. Dye it to the required shade, then give it an individual touch by stamping it with an attractive motif, such as the fleur-de-lys design shown here.*

◀ **Bedroom style** *A wicker bedroom chair has been given a new look with a cover-up made from a cotton bedspread. The fabric has been tucked under the seat and the four corners have been tied into loose single knots.*

▶ **Table tie** *Tables – whether improvised or the real thing – make perfect candidates for the cover-up craze. Cover the table with an extra-long piece of cloth, and knot it stylishly to one side, as shown.*

▲ **Summer swags** *A floor-length cloth has been swagged with muslin for a special occasion. Bunch the muslin at intervals and secure with rubber bands. Then pin the swag to the cloth from underneath.*

CLEVER CUSHIONS

*A scattering of creative cushions provides
the vital spark that lifts a room scheme. Make each cushion
a work of art by playing with contrasting fabrics,
eye-catching details and innovative trims.*

*Each of these cushions
has its own quirky
design which attracts and
delights the eye. As a group,
they create a burst of colour.*

Traditional frilled or piped cushions in coordinated fabrics are a safe option in any room, but why not use cushions to introduce fresh, unexpected fabrics and design ideas into your home? A cushion can look twice as stylish if you make it from two or more eye-catching fabrics. You could create a cushion with an elaborate floral centre panel, bordered with a crisp, checked fabric; or make a half-and-half cushion by dividing it diagonally with two brightly coloured silks, or by using different fabrics for the front and back.

Try copying two of the cushions shown on the previous page by making an inner and an outer cover, and allowing the inner one to peep through – either at the sides, as on the checked cushion with the tie-on outer cover, or through tiny slits in the front, like the green and pink cushion.

If you want to brighten up existing cushions, appliqué them with motifs in contrasting fabrics. Large floral or paisley motifs look fabulous appliquéd on to plain, glazed cotton cushions.

TANTALIZING TRIMS

Make the most of a plain cushion by adding some innovative trims, such

Clever contrasts These cushions make a cheerful group. They're subtly coordinated in colour, yet each one has its own distinctive style. Splashy spots cover the top cushion, giving it a jolly look, while the rich checks of the bottom cushion have a far crisper, smarter feel. The white cushion in the middle balances the group and its tasselled trim reinforces the colour link.

Doily display
Delicately crocheted motifs look charming appliquéd on to cushion fronts. Here, the motifs have been worked in soft rust and grey yarns to match their crisp gingham backgrounds perfectly. You can copy this look by dyeing shop-bought doilies to match your cushion fabric.

as quirky buttons, wool or raffia tufts, silky tassels or even sparkling sequins. Scour home furnishing shops and department stores for inspiration.

Colourful ribbons can look fabulous tied casually around plain cushions, like the ones in the picture above. Alternatively, you could stitch ribbons around the edges of a cushion to create decorative borders. You can use braids in the same way to give cushions a sumptuous, textured finish. Russia braid or narrow, flexible gimp looks good stitched on in swirling designs.

Lots of ready-made trimmings can be jazzed up with a creative touch. Try stitching deep fringing around the edges of a cushion, then bead some of the strands, knotting them under the beads to hold them in place. Use thick fringing and chunky wooden beads for a lounge cushion, and fine, ivory silk fringing threaded with pearls and crystals in the bedroom. Or you could trim a simple gingham cushion with broderie anglaise edging, then thread the broderie anglaise with fine ribbon to match the fabric.

▲ *Ribbon riot* *Sumptuous silk cushions in jewel colours will lift your spirits on the greyest of days, and can bring a room to life. These cushions have been given a witty and glamorous finish with lengths of gauzy ribbon tied around them, so they resemble exotic gifts. You can buy sheer flat or ruched ribbons in many colours, with contrasting or self patterns.*

▶ *Victorian delicacy* *Hand-worked cushion covers, like the one shown here, have a charm and nostalgia all of their own. Here, the cover is made from squares of crisp white lawn, interspersed with squares of dainty cobweb crochet lace. An exquisitely embroidered floral motif adorns alternate squares of lawn.*

Traditional textiles *These softly toning cushions are strong on texture and gentle on colour. They combine rich tapestry and damask fabrics with traditional trimmings. You can recreate this look by stitching a wide tapestry-effect border down the centre or sides of a jacquard, velvet or damask cushion, and trimming it with cord, fringing or tasselled braid.*

Patch it up *Patchwork cushions have a comforting feel which makes a room more inviting. The two shown here are made from blue and white mini-print fabrics to match their surroundings. One shows a cottage, and the other a star motif.*

Modern mood *Simple trimmings give these cushions a bright, modern look. On the checked cushion, outsized fabric-covered buttons in singing yellow stand out dramatically against the red background and highlight the yellow stripe in the fabric. The cushion is trimmed with matching yellow piping.*

The white cushion cover has a fun finish with boldly coloured tassels, stitched on to the front and corners. You can make tassels like these yourself from silky strands of embroidery cotton.

WRAPPED CUSHIONS

A length of fabric, a few yards of ribbon and some cord can give your old cushions a fresh new look or create designer transformations for plain ready-made ones.

You can make cushions to match your curtains or to cheer up a tired room scheme with a minimum of effort and no sewing. The method is simple – it involves wrapping cushion pads in fabrics and tying them firmly in place with ribbon or cord, or wrapping a plain cushion with a colourful scarf or length of fabric for an even simpler but effective cushion idea.

You can cover cushions of all shapes and sizes, and because you are simply using lengths of fabric you can change your covers whenever you want to create a different look. For a classic effect you might choose a rich brocade or heavy silk tied with gold cord; for an exotic flavour, you could try wrapping the cushion with an ethnic Ikat or Navajo-style fabric, and secure it with chunky natural rope or raffia; or for a romantic-style room, you could layer voile or lace over ready-made cushions and tie

Golden wraps Give your cushions a quick party look by wrapping them in glittering metallic fabric and tying them up with matching cords. Here, a bolster was wrapped in turquoise gauze and a layer of gold mesh, then its ends were fastened with gold cord. The square cushion was wrapped in metallic fabric and silk flowers were tied in place parcel-style with ivory silk cords. Upholstery webbing holds the ends of the check fabric bolster firmly in place (right).

the fabric in place with ribbon – the possibilities are endless.

To neaten edges, either press under a hem and secure it with fusible webbing, or use deckle-edged scissors.

Scarf facelift If your scarf drawer is overflowing, put the contents to good use by using scarves to give plain cushions a lift. Choose cotton or silky textures depending on the look you want. Fold bright cotton squares crosswise to give the maximum length and knot them round your cushion. Longer scarves give you more design options.

Leather thongs All kinds of materials are suitable for tying your cushions. In this contemporary sitting room, cushions adopt a rustic look with ties made of soft leather thongs, available from craft shops.

Buttoned up Cut fabric squares the same size as your cushions and press under the raw edges using fusible webbing. Position the squares diagonally on the back and front of the cushion and fasten the four corners with buttons.

Romantic lace Collect crisp white lace-edged linen, and create no-sew cushion covers. Here, antimacassars and bread basket liners were used to make these pretty cushions. Simply place one fabric piece on either side of the cushion pad, then thread baby ribbon through both lace edges to tie the pieces together.

EASY APPLIQUÉ CUSHIONS

Use up those scraps of fabric that are too good to throw away by transforming plain cushions with imaginative and easy-to-make fabric appliqués.

Making your own soft furnishings usually means you are left with fabric scraps that are too good to throw away but not quite big enough to make into anything else. You can use these scraps to make quick and easy, iron-on fabric appliqués to transform plain cushion covers into designer cushions.

Look for fabrics in contrasting colours and textures that work with your cushion covers. Then think about a design for the appliqué and make a template if necessary. Simple shapes are not only the easiest, they are the most effective. You can add details later with beads and braids.

Draw your appliqué design on the paper backing of the fusible webbing. Cut this out and iron it to the wrong side of the appliqué fabric. Cut out through all layers along the drawn line. To stick your design on to the cushion cover, peel away the backing and iron into position.

Shapes of summer
Choose crisp white and natural linen cushions and add delicate voile appliqués in bright colours for a smart summer look. The rims of different sized wine glasses were used as templates for the circles, and the random squares were fringed before being bonded to the cushion.

Tulip touch *Checks and florals are a classic combination, the neat grid design of the one perfectly complementing the free-flowing lines of the other. Cut out single flower motifs from a floral print fabric, and appliqué them on to ready-made checked cushions.*

Animal magic *Get in safari mood with a children's jungle print in bright primary colours. Either cut the animals out – you could cut round them using deckle-edged scissors – or cut out a square incorporating an animal, as here, pressing under the raw edges before bonding to the cushion.*

Checkmate *Have some fun with checked cushions by making appliqués in contrasting checks. Here, brightly coloured checked fabrics have been used to make sharply tailored or more casually fringed appliqué squares.*

Visions in velvet *Cut out graphic shapes of fruit and butterflies from velvet, using deckle-edged scissors, and bond them to simple Indian ribbed-cotton cushions. As a finishing touch, add beads, braids and sequin highlights using clear craft adhesive.*

LACY EFFECTS

*Use lacy fabrics to create dreamy bedrooms
and Victorian-style drawing rooms, and scatter
lace-trimmed accessories around your home
for a fresh and feminine look.*

▼ *Give a window a dreamy
air with generous drapes
in ivory lace, trimmed with
deep lace frills and hung from
a slender iron pole.*

The term 'lace' is used to describe a whole range of exquisite openwork fabrics, from the genuine hand-worked article, such as needlepoint or bobbin lace, to crocheted and knitted lace and the machine-made lace that's so widely available. It also includes whitework embroidery, such as broderie anglaise, drawn thread work, hardanger and cutwork.

◀ **Doily detail** *Soften the lines of a striped cushion by stitching a knitted lace doily on to the front. Complete the effect with a simple border of fabric, like the narrow striped border shown here, which acts as a frame for the lace.*

You'll find all these different types of lace in specialist fabric shops and large sewing stores. Antique lace is expensive and tends to be very fragile, but you can recreate its mellow, aged feel by soaking a pretty machine-made lace in cold tea. You can then use it in abundance to create frothy window treatments and romantic bed drapes.

Hand-worked lace also tends to be pricey, so it's an excellent idea to try making some yourself – crocheted lace edgings for cushions or bedlinen, and knitted lace panels, which you can inset into tablecloths or curtains, are relatively simple projects for a beginner.

▶ *White nights* White, lacy bedlinen looks crisp and fresh, but it can be quite expensive. As an alternative, capture the charm of lace by investing in a few lace-trimmed cushions or pillows to scatter over your bed.

Look out for lacy fabrics and edgings on clothes and soft furnishings at jumble sales and charity shops, where you can sometimes find exquisite pieces at bargain prices. Even damaged pieces can be recycled: you can salvage the good parts and use them for appliqué, insets or small projects.

LACE IN THE HOME

You can use lace in your home in small touches or with gay abandon, depending on the effect you want to create. If you like the romantic, dreamy look created by yards and yards of lace, indulge yourself in the bedroom, where you can cover every surface with lace. Go for floor-length lace drapes and a lacy valance at the windows, teamed with lace-trimmed bedlinen. Make a lacy skirt for your dressing table and buy plenty of lace-trimmed accessories, such as clothes hangers and scented sachets.

Touches of lace in the dining room or living room can look crisp and smart, as well as pretty. Make a stiffened lace roller blind and team it with formal curtains – the lace will cast dancing shadows across the room as daylight filters through. Trim the curtain tiebacks with a lace edging to complete the look, and treat yourself to a lacy runner to protect the surface of a polished wooden table.

Use lace panels over small windows in bathrooms and cloakrooms – their pattern will be silhouetted against the light, and they'll give daytime privacy.

◀ *Lacy topcloth* Drape a length of elegant curtain lace over a plain, coloured tablecloth to recreate this charming tea-time setting. The dainty paisley motifs on the lace show up well against the soft green background of the undercloth. The scalloped side edges of the lace hang prettily just above the floor, while the raw ends are simply tucked under out of sight.

▶ *On the shelf* Glue dainty crocheted lace edgings to the front of cupboard shelves to soften their hard edges and add a homey, cottage style feel.

▶ *Hand-crafted charm*
Hexagonal inserts of fine,
knitted lace have been stitched
along the bottom of this white
cotton curtain. The intricacy
of the lacy panels stands out
against the light, and the
strong weave of the curtain
fabric emphasizes their
fragility. The lower edge of
the curtain has been shaped
into a zigzag to echo the lines
of the inserts.

To copy this look, position
each lace insert on the curtain
and trace round it with a
dressmakers' pen. Remove
the inserts and cut away the
curtain fabric 2cm (¾in)
inside the edge of the drawn
shape. Neaten the raw fabric
edges with zigzag stitches,
and press 1cm (⅜in) to the
right side around the edges,
snipping into the turnings
for ease, as necessary.
Topstitch the lace in place
on the curtain, covering
the turnings.

▲ *Lacy accessories* Lace-trimmed accessories, like these
bedroom hangers, always look fresh and pretty. You can
buy lacy hangers ready-made, or trim plain white padded coat-
hangers with lace – there are lots of lovely trims to choose from.

◀ *Colour splash* Colourful crocheted lace makes a lively
alternative to white or ivory lace. These edgings were worked
by hand in navy blue, cream, red and pink to match the
cushions, but you could simply dye white or ivory, machine-
made edgings to match your cushions.

BOW TRIMS

Versatile bows, tied from ribbon or fabric, lend an instant flourish to home furnishings and accessories. Make them simple or lavish, depending on your taste.

Casually knotted in single loops, or shaped into full layers with generous trailing ends, a bow adds instant decorative appeal to home furnishings. Perch dainty bows on top of picture frames or tie them round slender lampbases; or glue tiny silk ribbon bows on to a lampshade for an exquisite finishing touch. Add a flourish to cushions and bedlinen with full bow trims stitched in place; or create lavish curtain tiebacks with broad fabric strips or wide ribbons tied in chunky bows around the drapes.

You can make bows in a number of ways and styles. Ribbon bows are usually tied from one continuous length, while fabric bows are generally assembled from two or three seamed tubes of material, stitched together to form a neat bow. A bow may be single-loop or multi-loop – where the material is folded concertina-style until the desired number of loops have been made, then pinched in the middle and stitched or wired to hold the loops and tails in place.

Opulent bow
Create a lavish bow from a remnant of silky fabric. Cut the fabric into wide strips and seam the edges to make tubes, then press flat. Shape the tubes into loops for the bow and use another strip to make the tails. Wind a length of wire tightly round the middle to hold the bow together.

Hops and bows
Cheerful yellow and white check bows bring a fresh look to a rustic swag of dried hops draped over a window. Each single-loop bow is tied from a continuous strip of fabric and wired in position. A matching bow on top of a picture frame continues the theme. You could cut the fabric strips using deckle edge scissors to give the bows a decorative finish.

Double the style This double-loop bow is made from one piece of ribbon, folded concertina-style then wired in the middle to hold the loops and tails in place. Wrap the longer tail round the neck of the bow to conceal the wire.

Picture perfect Hang nursery prints on the wall using lengths of ribbon and picture nails; then trim each ribbon with a dainty ribbon bow, positioned to conceal the nails.

Dressing up A bright chair cover is given a theatrical finishing touch with large fabric bows at the top of each leg. Make each bow from a long strip of fabric, cut on the bias and sewn into a tube to conceal the raw edges, then pressed flat. For a tailored look, assemble the bow from fabric tubes of varying lengths – one for the loops, one for the tails and a short strip for the knot – and stitch them together in a bow shape.

Spring idea Tie single-loop ribbon bows to a large, leafy house plant and hang painted Easter eggs from its branches to create a charming springtime decoration.

Pots of style Wrap an old plant holder in colourful fabric and trim it with a matching fabric bow to create an original and stylish accessory. The fabric for the pot and bow is first soaked in PVA adhesive so it will stiffen as it dries. Cover the pot first, then stick on the bow.

TIEBACK IDEAS

Sweep your drapes into shape with an instant curtain tieback.
Try a swirl of fake flowers, a length of fabric or a coil of rope – you can
add style and shape without sewing a single stitch.

Tiebacks make the perfect finishing touch for any window treatment. Their job is simply to hold back curtains, but with a little imagination, flair and ingenuity, they can inject much needed colour or design into a mundane room scheme.

It couldn't be easier – just take a scrap of fabric, a sprig of artificial flowers or berries, or a length of cord, and knot it in place. You could pep up a pair of plain or textured curtains with a scrap of treasured fabric or a favourite scarf. Try out unconventional materials – loosely twisted raffia looks great tied round brightly checked or striped curtains, and netting makes an unusual but effective choice to restrain billowing voile.

Try to suit the tieback to the room. Use sumptuous trims in your sitting room and dining room, and keep fun findings, such as shells, for bathrooms and bedrooms.

Stylish silk For simple elegance, tie brightly coloured silk scarves round sheer floor-length curtains. Here, two or three scarves in sea greens and blues have been used for each curtain. Fasten the scarves in floppy bows so that light both floods into the room and filters through the curtain fabric.

Simply Scandinavian *Sometimes the simplest ideas are the best. Here, the sheer central curtain is tied with fine white cord, while thin raffia bows hold back the outer gingham curtains. This clean, simple look is pure Scandinavian, softened only by the fabric falling in folds on the bare floorboards.*

Dramatic effect *Artificial berries and leaves make an elaborate tieback for a formal brocade curtain. This tieback is surprisingly easy to make. Gather up the curtain with a length of strong wire, looping it round a holding hook on the wall behind. Wrap dense sprays of plastic berries and silk leaves round the wire to create a sumptuous, theatrical arrangement.*

Seaside memories
Bring the seashore back home with an unexpected touch of glamour. Cut a wide strip of gold net and lay a selection of shells along its length. Wrap the net around the shells and staple the long edges together. Loop the net round the curtain and tie an elaborate bow at the back, fixing the tieback on to a holding hook on the wall. Arrange the shells at the front of the tieback until you are satisfied with the result.

HOLDBACK IDEAS

The contrasting texture of wood or metal holdbacks
set against gently draped curtains adds a stylish
finish to any window. For a truly coordinated look,
match them to your pole.

Holdbacks are rigid fittings made of metal or wood which do exactly as their name suggests – they hold the curtain back from the window, allowing in as much daylight as possible, while also keeping the folds of the curtains in place. They offer an exciting range of alternatives to fabric or rope tiebacks, and add a distinctive style to your room.

Holdbacks have a more formal look than tiebacks, and are very easy to fit. There are a number of different types for you to choose from, all of which give you the opportunity to dress your curtains into elegant, curving folds. All

▲ **Colour matched** *The blue stain of these holdbacks has been chosen to accentuate the colours of the curtains.*

holdbacks look better if you draw the curtains across at the top a bit to give fullness to the drape, rather than pulling them right back to the sides.

Instant effect *A spare lined curtain has been used in this bedroom to create an attractive tented effect. Fix a short pole at right angles to the wall above the bed, drape the curtain over it and arrange the fabric round the bed head as desired.*

Tropical nights *Give a minimally styled room a touch of drama with a mosquito net canopy made from sheer fabric. The simplicity of the canopy is perfectly in keeping with the room's fresh, pared-down colour scheme.*

Country romance *Delicately patterned lace makes the perfect bed drape for a country-style room. The tented effect here has been achieved by attaching the fabric to different points in the sloping ceiling, then fanning it out on either side.*

Classic elegance *Coordinate your bed drape with your room scheme. Here, a drape with a sumptuous bow at the top echoes the colour of the walls and soft furnishings and the design of the bedcover. Large matching bows on the bed posts complete the effect.*

HOLDBACK IDEAS

*The contrasting texture of wood or metal holdbacks
set against gently draped curtains adds a stylish
finish to any window. For a truly coordinated look,
match them to your pole.*

Holdbacks are rigid fittings made of metal or wood which do exactly as their name suggests – they hold the curtain back from the window, allowing in as much daylight as possible, while also keeping the folds of the curtains in place. They offer an exciting range of alternatives to fabric or rope tiebacks, and add a distinctive style to your room.

Holdbacks have a more formal look than tiebacks, and are very easy to fit. There are a number of different types for you to choose from, all of which give you the opportunity to dress your curtains into elegant, curving folds. All

▲ *Colour matched The blue stain of these holdbacks has been chosen to accentuate the colours of the curtains.*

holdbacks look better if you draw the curtains across at the top a bit to give fullness to the drape, rather than pulling them right back to the sides.

Versatile holdbacks

Sun struck *Let the sun shine in by drawing your curtains back with this shiny brass, embrace-style holdback.*

Colour match *Natural wood holdbacks can be easily stained to match or contrast with your colour scheme.*

Brass class *Sumptuous red damask and intricate brass give an air of luxury and traditional comfort.*

Feather sweep *A slender embrace, shaped like a long feather, teams well with heavily fringed curtains.*

Going green *The soft patina of verdigris on an ornately worked metal holdback adds detail to simple trellis fabric.*

Similar motifs *A bronze rose accentuates the pattern of a rose-strewn fabric without disturbing its quiet tones.*

Simple lines *A spiral of wrought iron echoes a popular pole finial and adds character to the simplest of fabrics.*

Classically inspired *In rich brass, a classic embrace, shaped like a furled leaf, looks suitably formal for a brocade drape.*

Iron will *Forged iron is one of the most fashionable choices for modern-style embraces – and comes in many designs.*

EASY SWAGS AND TAILS

*By draping fabric over a pole or other fixture you can
create a quick and easy window treatment that will
transform your room.*

Easy swags, or scarf drapes, are the simplest form of window treatment to make. A length of fabric is simply tied or draped from a curtain pole, or from special curtain accessories such as valance creators, holdbacks or scarf rings, all available from department stores and soft furnishing shops.

These curtain fixtures are attached with screws to the wall above and to either side of the window. Using scarf rings you can create extra flourishes such as rosettes and Bishops' sleeves,

by pulling the swag fabric through the ring and twisting it into the desired shape.

Choose a lightweight fabric, and use the whole width of the material. Neaten the ends with fusible webbing or fray the edges of an open weave fabric into a fringe. Look out for beautiful finished textile pieces such as large shawls, bedspreads or lace cloths. For lined drapes place two pieces of fabric with right sides together, stitch around the sides, leaving a small gap. Then turn the fabric

▲ Elegantly understated
Embroidered muslin is loosely knotted around a plain wooden curtain pole and then draped over the ends to form short tails. A pair of matt white louvred shutters complete the relaxed café-style setting.

right side out and slipstitch closed.

When measuring up for the fabric, remember to allow extra for any knots and twists. If necessary, practise first using an old length of material to judge how much fabric you need.

▶ *Country cottage creation*
A length of checked cotton is knotted around a pair of valance creators – metal spirals screwed on to the wall above the window. The ends of the fabric are cut straight, hanging like curtains to the sill and framing a chintz roller blind, for a rustic look.

▼ *The extravagant touch* *A length of silk taffeta-lined dupion is draped over an ornate brass curtain pole. It has been teamed with a matching silk gauze London blind and cotton muslin curtains. As an opulent finishing touch, streamers of lined dupion, tied in bows, hang from the ends of the pole.*

▼ *Ringing in a change* *Scarf rings are versatile gadgets that allow you to arrange a swag into a variety of different shapes and styles. Here, a large floral print cotton fabric has been twisted and drawn through the central ring and then knotted through the outer rings, allowing the ends to hang down to frame the window. The drapery adds movement and colour to a simple cream roller blind, creating a cheerful, sunny mood.*

ARRANGING A SWAG

If you have a curtain pole, you can create an instant swag – just drape a length of fabric over the top of the pole and secure it at the back with tacks or staples. Let the ends of the swag hang down on either side of the window to create a soft frame. You won't need to stitch the fabric unless it frays easily – in that case, just hem the raw edges.

On a narrow window, the fabric looks best arranged in a single swag, but you can have two swags on a standard window, caught at the middle by a fabric tie or wrapped once round the pole. Emphasize wide windows by wrapping fabric several times round the pole. This reveals the back of the fabric, so use either a sheer

Curtain and lining fabrics are looped around a pole and left to fall gracefully to the floor. A few tacks secure the fabric to the back of the pole.

or a plain fabric which looks the same on both sides. Alternatively, fold the fabric in half with the wrong sides together so that these don't show. This creates a very neat effect.

If you don't have a curtain pole, it's still easy to put up a swag. Attach light or mediumweight fabric to decorative hooks on either side of the window, or use valance creators. These are special coils which will hold the fabric neatly at the top of a window. Or, if there's an architrave round the window, you can even fix your swag to the top of this.

Sheer delight *Create this elegant asymmetrical arrangement by twisting sheer fabric around a curtain pole. Knot the top of the fabric on to the pole and add a few tacks at the back to secure it.*

Light touch *Just two small hooks are all that's needed to hold this lightweight window drape in place. The drape lets in lots of light, while cutting out the glare.*

Perfect balance *A striped seersucker swag adds a jaunty touch to a small window. The fabric is pulled through valance creators at each side of the window and scrunched into rosettes.*

QUICK BED DRAPES

Crown your bed with a length of fabric, softly draped from a pole or hoop, to create an elegant focal point in your bedroom.

You can arrange simple fabric drapes in a variety of ways to form an attractive triangular or tented effect at the head of your bed. Hang fabric from a curtain pole fixed flush to the wall, or fix a short pole at right angles to it and drape fabric over it. Or use valance creators, holdbacks or scarf rings and attach them to the wall or ceiling and to either side of the bed. Add fabric bows or rosettes to conceal the fixtures.

Alternatively, fix a canopy above the bed so that the fabric fans out from a hoop at the top. You can make your own canopy using a large lampshade ring or embroidery hoop and lengths of fabric; or use an easy-to-assemble kit, available from department stores or soft furnishings shops.

Use lightweight curtain fabrics that drape well. Delicate sheers create a light, airy effect, while muslin, calico or cotton lining are very economical. Select a fabric that looks good from both sides and simply hem the edges. Or add extra impact by lining drapes with a contrasting fabric – you could even recycle an old lined curtain that matches your room scheme.

When measuring up, use the whole width of fabric and allow extra length for any knots and twists. Secure the drapes on either side of the bed with tiebacks or holdbacks or allow them to sweep freely to the floor.

▼ *Simply stylish A length of muslin, draped casually over a wrought-iron curtain pole and loosely knotted at each end, gives a fresh, modern look to this traditional bedroom.*

➤ **Instant effect** *A spare lined curtain has been used in this bedroom to create an attractive tented effect. Fix a short pole at right angles to the wall above the bed, drape the curtain over it and arrange the fabric round the bed head as desired.*

◄ **Tropical nights** *Give a minimally styled room a touch of drama with a mosquito net canopy made from sheer fabric. The simplicity of the canopy is perfectly in keeping with the room's fresh, pared-down colour scheme.*

➤ **Country romance** *Delicately patterned lace makes the perfect bed drape for a country-style room. The tented effect here has been achieved by attaching the fabric to different points in the sloping ceiling, then fanning it out on either side.*

◄ **Classic elegance** *Coordinate your bed drape with your room scheme. Here, a drape with a sumptuous bow at the top echoes the colour of the walls and soft furnishings and the design of the bedcover. Large matching bows on the bed posts complete the effect.*

IMPROVISED HEADBOARDS

*With a little imagination you can create an inexpensive
headboard for your bed from found objects, giving your
bedroom a touch of individuality and instant style.*

A headboard gives a bed distinction, defining its space and focusing attention on the largest and most important piece of furniture in the room. Traditional headboards are made of polished wood or are luxuriously padded and covered with fabric to match the soft furnishings; but they are often expensive and so are frequently dispensed with altogether. However, a headboard does make the bed a cosier place, protecting you from draughts and providing support for your pillows. It also protects the wallcovering behind.

With an imaginative eye, you can convert everyday objects into instant headboards and give your bedroom a unique style. For a rustic look, your local garden centre is a good place to start. Look for woven willow fencing, available in numerous widths and heights. You can leave it natural or spray paint it for a more finished appearance.

Fabric makes another good bedhead. You could attach cushions or suspend a quilt or small rug from a curtain pole, and install it at the appropriate height. To work this out, sit on the bed, leaning back against the wall to mark the most comfortable height for you.

An architectural salvage yard may provide you with a discarded iron gate or a piece of fencing that would make a spectacular headboard.

▼ ***Cut adrift*** *An interesting piece of wood, perhaps from a barrel or an old boat, cut to a rough shape and mounted on the wall, makes a unique rustic headboard for a cottage bedroom. Make sure you clean the wood gently but thoroughly, to remove dirt. You could then apply a matt varnish for further protection without losing the character of the old wood.*

Garden fence The warm look of woven willow fencing makes a charming country-style headboard. Fencing comes in various dimensions and can be wedged firmly between the bed and the wall. You could paint it or leave it natural.

Cushioned comfort Turn ready-made cushions tied at the side into a comfortable padded bedhead. Install a decorative curtain pole above the bed and tie on as many cushions as you need.

Architectural salvage Discarded wrought-iron railings found in a builder's yard, rival any antique bedstead for a fraction of the price. Use a wire brush to clean off any rust and dirt and then spray paint the metal if desired.

Cosy quilt Fold a softly patterned quilt over a rail installed above the bed for a cosy bedhanging. You could use other fabrics such as an antique curtain, small oriental rug or decorative throw, in the same way. Make sure the rail is substantial enough to support the weight of the fabric draped over it.

DISPLAYING FOUND OBJECTS

Look out for interesting objects that have been discarded or can be picked up for next to nothing in a junk shop, and turn them into imaginative decorations for your home.

You can find unusual items in the most unexpected places – on a walk in the country or town, at the beach, or at a local garage sale. Train your eye to spot objects with interesting shapes, colours and textures and then think about how you might display or group them.

Nature throws away unwanted items all the time – shells whose occupants have long gone, seedpods, rocks, pine cones and odd-shaped branches. Use them to decorate accessories or simply arrange them in a pleasing way – fill a glass jar with colourful pebbles, for instance, or create pictures with dried leaves.

Items that other people have abandoned might also catch your eye. Look in architectural salvage yards for pieces of intricate moulding or wrought iron, which can have a new life as decorations. Junk shops and garage sales are also good hunting grounds for collectibles such as saucer-less teacups, pottery jars or old glass bottles.

▼ ***Nature's store*** *Exotic and intricate shapes abound in the natural world. Here, spiralling organic shapes have inspired a collection of objects and pictures displayed in pale wood frames.*

Kitchen corner Hold on to attractive empty oil bottles or old-fashioned stoneware food containers, and combine them with wooden kitchen equipment for a rustic themed window display.

Labels for less Soak off interesting wine labels and arrange them on a piece of framed coloured card or mounting board as a souvenir of memorable occasions and happy holidays.

Old-time advertising Unusual metal advertising plaques create this colourful wall display. Keep an eye out in markets and junk shops for items that might make an interesting collection.

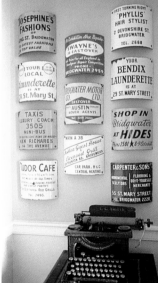

Musical duo Don't discard an old piece of furniture before checking it for good parts that can be re-cycled. Here, the panels holding brass candleholders have been removed from the front of an old family piano and lovingly restored. The result is a pair of elegant wall sconces.

Versatile containers Some fine wines are still shipped in wooden boxes. Ask your wine merchant for any unwanted attractive boxes stamped with images of vineyards and French chateaux, and use them to create original containers for plants.

DÉCOUPAGED LAMP BASE

*Turn a plain glass lamp base into a beautiful accessory for
your home. Using the simple techniques of
découpage, paste cut-out paper motifs
to the inside of the lamp base.*

*This lovely lamp base
was originally clear
glass. Paper flowers were
stuck to the inside, and the
background painted blue.*

This method of decorating a glass lamp base with cut-out paper motifs is just like ordinary découpage, but with two important differences. On glass, the motifs are stuck to the inside of the object, instead of the outside. Then you just need to add a couple of coats of paint and varnish, instead of the many layers of varnish that ordinary découpage requires.

CHOOSING MOTIFS

You'll find interesting motifs on giftwrap and wallpaper; or you can use motifs from magazines, photocopies, pictures from old books and damaged prints; or you can buy them from craft stores. Try to collect motifs with a theme, such as shells, flowers, geometric shapes or animals.

The best motifs for découpage have clearly defined outlines – this makes them easier to cut out. They should also be strong enough to withstand wetting with adhesive and paint without tearing or disintegrating.

CHOOSING A LAMP BASE

You will need a plain glass lamp base with a wide base opening. Make sure that you can fit your hand inside to stick on the cut-outs and to paint and varnish it.

MATERIALS

Glass lamp base with a wide base opening

Paper motifs

Sharp pointed scissors or craft knife

Spray fixative

PVA adhesive

Water-based paint

Small paintbrush

China marking crayon

Clear varnish

Tweezers (optional)

Acrylic putty (Blu-tac)

Plastic sheeting

Damp cloth

Small piece of sponge

Coloured pencils (optional)

PREPARING THE MOTIFS

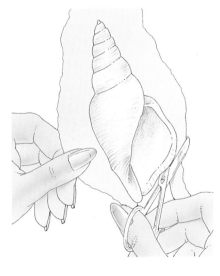

1 CUTTING OUT THE MOTIFS
If necessary, draw round each motif with a matching coloured pencil to mark the cutting line. Roughly cut around the motif, then trim around the outline, holding the scissors at a slight angle to give the paper a bevelled edge. This helps the paper to blend with the background.

Cut more motifs than you think you will need so that you have plenty to choose from when trying out different arrangements and effects.

2 SEALING THE MOTIFS
Lay out your paper motifs face down on the plastic sheeting and spray the wrong side with spray fixative to prevent them becoming transparent when they are wet. Make sure the motifs don't stick to the sheeting. If you are using thin paper, such as giftwrap, allow the sealer to dry, then spray the other side as well.

DECORATING THE BASE

1 ARRANGING THE MOTIFS
Arrange your paper cut-outs on the outside of the lamp base – use acrylic putty to secure them. Handle the motifs carefully, and use tweezers to hold fragile shapes. If you wish to see how the lamp base will look when the background has been painted, place a piece of paper – the same colour as the background paint – inside the base.

2 MARKING THE POSITIONS
When you are happy with your arrangement, use a china crayon to draw round the motifs on the outside of the glass. Number each position and the corresponding motif, so you know exactly where to place each one.

◄ This gorgeous lamp base was decorated with motifs cut from wrapping paper and then painted blue. The shade didn't coordinate with the base, so it was lightly sprayed with gold paint to match the motifs.

3 APPLYING THE MOTIFS
Using the small paintbrush, apply adhesive to the front of your first motif. Position it inside the lamp base and gently smooth it flat with a damp cloth. Take care not to over-wet the paper. Use the cloth to press out any air bubbles from under the paper – they will show up when the adhesive is dry. Wipe away the excess adhesive, then stick on the other motifs in the same way. Wipe off the china crayon outlines.

4 PAINTING THE BACKGROUND
When the motifs are dry, use the sponge to pat an even coat of paint all over the back of the glass, and leave it to dry for 24 hours. Apply a second coat of paint and leave it to dry.

5 APPLYING THE VARNISH
Paint a thin layer of varnish over the paint to seal it, and leave it to dry. Apply a second coat of varnish.

FANCIFUL LAMPSHADES

*Take a plain lampshade as your starting point and let your
imagination run riot. Decorate it with colourful trimmings,
everlasting flowers or pressed leaves.*

Liven up a lampshade with inexpensive decorations
from around your home. You can use decorations
to add pattern or texture, change the profile of the
shade or add colour when the lamp is lit. On these pages
there are some suggestions that will suit various room
styles and settings, and perhaps inspire you to experiment with your own ideas.

Craft or PVA adhesive is suitable for sticking on most
decorative items. For delicate fabrics use a specialist
fabric adhesive and for heavier items, made from glass,
plastic or metal, use an epoxy resin adhesive. Both fabric
and paper lampshades are suitable for decorating. You
may wish to further embellish your instant decorations
by lacing the edges of the shade with leather thonging,
ribbon or raffia. When adding decorations that overlap
the edges of the shade, make sure they are safely away
from the light bulb.

▲ *Neutral and natural Stick parcel string or garden
twine on a plain shade to create an updated rustic look.
Loop the string along the upper and lower edges of the
shade, sticking it in place as you go with small dots of
adhesive. Or stick pressed leaves randomly over the shade
(below) then accentuate the edges with leather thonging.*

Creative collage *A paper lampshade is the perfect base for a simple collage which combines colours, interesting images and unusual textures to create an artistic effect. Use favourite clippings, old stamps, photographs or pictures; or base the collage on a theme, such as a holiday, hobby, or historical event.*

Lacy outline *A length of ornamental antique lace makes a pretty, petticoat-like addition to a plain or patterned lampshade. Secure the lace to the lower inside edge of the shade so the cutwork pattern is shown in silhouette when the lamp is illuminated.*

Floral fancy *Stems of everlasting anemones trim this eye-catching shade, bringing the cheerful colours of the cottage garden indoors. Green foliage, twined at the upper and lower edge of the shade, provide an edging for the flowers.*

Satin bands *For a delicate finishing touch, add bands of satin ribbon and miniature ribbon bows to a simple shade. Hold the ends of the ribbon temporarily in place with pieces of masking tape, until you are pleased with the spacing, then secure them with adhesive on the wrong side of the shade. Pinch in the satin bands at intervals with tiny bows.*

ROPE TRICKS

*Let natural rope and string play a decorative as well as a
practical role in your home, by using them as textured trimmings
and finishing details on furnishings and accessories.*

Synthetic fibres and sticky tapes have largely taken over the role of natural rope and string in parcel wrapping. But far from becoming redundant, these natural materials have taken on a new lease of life in interior design.

Made from plant fibres, such as hemp and cotton, twisted together into various thicknesses, rope and string have definite sculptural appeal. With their pleasing earthy colours and crunchy textures, they can be used to create and enhance natural-style accessories and soft furnishings in your home.

Try using thick, bleached white cotton rope or cord for accessories such as tiebacks for linen and plain fabric curtains. You could also loop a length of it across the top of a window to soften the starkness of plain roller blinds in a modern room scheme.

Thin, strong white cotton kitchen string makes an unusual embroidery thread for coarse fabrics, or you can wrap it round cushions. Garden twines and twisted rush cords are the perfect choice for decorating lamp bases and shades, for example. You could even pile together a collection of balls of string and garden twines as a soft, sculptural alternative to fruit or flowers.

▼ On the ropes
*The natural
colours of rope, string
and twine work well in
simple, contemporary
room schemes. Use
these fibrous cords to
coil round lampbases,
decorate cushions or to
add a finishing touch
to a window treatment.*

▼ **All caught up** *Fabrics made of natural fibres are perfect for a casual room scheme. Here, a cotton throw is harnessed to a chair with knotted rope, which also trims the blind. To complete the look, narrower string is used to add textural detailing to plain cushions.*

▲ **Rope on board** *A piece of timber with a rope trim makes an unusual headboard. Use a glue gun to secure the end of the rope behind the board then wind it tightly round the board several times, finishing off with the rope out of sight behind the board. Hold the rope in place at intervals along the board, as necessary, with dabs of glue.*

▲ **Nautical loops** *The crisp good looks of white cotton window shades provide privacy without blocking out too much light. To soften the starkness, a length of chunky white cotton rope has been looped across the window and its ends tied in chunky knots.*

▶ **Garden green** *Thick green garden string has been used to enhance a plain lamp. Wrap the string tightly round the lampbase using PVA adhesive to hold the rows of string in place. For the lampshade trim, twirl a continuous length of string into loops and stick each one in place.*

Button Collection

Use bright buttons as trims for a range of home accessories. They're quick to sew or stick in place for an instant splash of colour.

Button detail
A line of large self-cover buttons, covered with remnants of saffron silk and placed along the cushion's envelope opening, add a designer detail to this checked cushion cover.

Mirror, mirror *Create instant sparkle on a mirror by gluing a medley of bright buttons, sequins and dazzling gemstones on to its frame. This frame was first covered with foil for added shine.*

If you're wondering what to do with all the odd buttons you've accumulated over the years, try using them as colourful trims for home accessories – from curtains and cushions to picture frames and lampshades.

Buttons are fun to collect, and generally not very expensive, so you can always supplement your own store with a few novel additions – unusually shaped buttons, such as triangles and stars, for example, or themed children's buttons. You can often buy odd buttons at flea markets and antique shops; and don't forget to recycle buttons from discarded clothes.

Pots of colour *Spray paint plain terracotta flowerpots in bright primary colours, and stick an assortment of different sized buttons evenly spaced round the rim. Use buttons to tone or contrast with the pot – either in different shades of the same colour, as with the purple and lilac buttons shown here, or in a vibrant mix of colours.*

Button contrast *Fabric-covered buttons in contrast colours add flair to soft furnishings, such as this cushion and pleated loose chair cover. To recreate the look on the chair cover, simply stitch a covered button to the top of each pleat.*

Bright and bold *A neat line of large, bright red buttons stitched along the border of a floral duvet cover adds a fun, contemporary note. The buttons are purely decorative, stitched to the top layer of fabric only, but you could easily use them as the fastening for a duvet cover that you're making yourself.*

Charming checks *Cheerful gingham scraps and simple white buttons add colour and country charm to plain lampshades. Cut out 7.5cm (3in) squares of gingham using pinking shears. Stick the fabric squares randomly on to the shade, and glue a large, plain white button in the centre of each one.*

BOX FRAMES

Deep box frames can be used to house a host of treasured possessions, from flowers saved from precious bouquets to tiny collections of shells and kitchen spices.

Treasured mementoes collected from weddings, birthdays and holidays all too often end up at the back of a drawer where they remain, forgotten until the next time you spring clean. But, rather than pushing your souvenirs out of sight, you can display them in a box frame – creating an heirloom that can be admired and cherished.

Box frames are also the perfect answer for displaying collections of interesting shells, stones, kitchen spices and other small objects that look good grouped together.

Remove the box frame backing and lay it flat to arrange the objects, then fit the frame and glass over your arrangement to view the effect. Once you're happy with the arrangement, stick the objects to the mounting board and reassemble the frame.

Some box frames, designed specifically for collections, come with small compartments. You can add wood or cardboard strips to divide a plain box frame in this way, or use an old-fashioned printer's tray which has ready-made dividers. Add picture rings and wire to the back to hang it on the wall.

Romantic roses Preserve the memory of a special occasion, such as a wedding or anniversary, by drying flowers from a bouquet and placing them in a box frame. Here, a pair of colourwashed frames contain simple rose arrangements. The glass fronts of the frames are decorated with fine handpainted lettering using glass or ceramic paint or rub-on transfers.

Seashore collection A printer's or collector's tray makes ideal storage for finds gleaned from the seashore. Seashells, pebbles, tiny starfish and sea lavender all fit perfectly in the tiny compartments. Rest the items on the ledges or stick them in place with double-sided adhesive foam pads.

Scrap-book souvenirs Clean-cut modern wooden frames are the perfect foil for treasured scraps. Torn pieces from manuscripts and music scores rub shoulders with photos and clever sayings. Use paper or craft adhesive to stick the pieces to the backing board, colour coordinating the entire composition or individual compartments within the frame.

Spice of life Whole spices often look too good for the pot! Instead, use a box frame to display a colourful arrangement. Cover the back of the frame with a piece of unbleached calico, then line up star anise, mace, nutmeg and cinnamon sticks to show off their interesting colours, textures and shapes. Stick dried chillies head-to-toe round the inside edges of the frame.

Congratulations! Create a wonderful present for a loving couple with a souvenir of their wedding day. Cover the bottom of the frame with wedding giftwrap and add mementoes of the special day – an invitation, a scrap of wedding dress fabric and lace, a champagne cork and a single dried bloom from the bouquet. Complete the display with a sprinkling of confetti.

SIMPLE FRAME IDEAS

*Use unusual trimmings to turn everyday picture frames into
something special. Fabric scraps, corrugated cardboard, even
postage stamps, can all be put to creative use.*

Custom-made and hand-decorated picture frames are expensive to buy – they're often works of art in their own right, embellished with trimmings that make each one unique. You can create your own exotic and original picture frames for a fraction of the price by adding a few decorations to simple ready-made frames. Choose a basic frame from a department or home furnishings store, or salvage an old frame if you have one lying around at home.

You can use all sorts of odds and ends for decorating the frame. For example, screws or upholstery nails will add glinting metallic highlights to bright, modern-look frames or frames in natural wood; dried flowers and strands of raffia have rustic appeal; scraps of pink, blue or yellow gingham and ribbon will create a charming frame for a child's picture.

Try out your design on the frame itself by roughly arranging the trimmings until you are happy with the effect. Then secure each piece individually with a glue gun or touch-and-close spots (Velcro discs). If the frame is fabric wrapped, you may need to have the glass recut to fit before completing the frame.

The result may be so spectacular that you can dispense with the picture altogether and use the frame as a piece of original artwork to stand on a mantelpiece or hang in a wall grouping, as shown left.

▲ **Frame composition** *Wrap inexpensive frames in scraps
of interesting fabric. You can hang the wrapped frames
empty as pieces of sculpture, or use them without glass as an
extension of the image they frame. For a snappy finishing
touch on a painted or smoothly covered frame, apply screws
or upholstery nails at intervals round the edges (right).*

Picture perfect *A range of materials and paint effects has been used to transform these plain picture frames and mounts into a coordinated grouping – including a ribbon bow, hand-painted scrolls, gilded detailing, card shapes and fine ribbon cross stitches.*

Daisy delight *Frame your latest holiday snaps in inexpensive painted frames, then make them just a little more original by adding outsize daisies (available from sewing stores) to the corners. Use a hot glue gun or touch-and-close spots to stick the motifs in place. For a bright finish, use craft paints to colour the daisy centres in summery shades.*

Stamp collection *Many postage stamps are so attractive they are worthy of being framed themselves. Show off their neat geometric shapes and bold colours by using them to decorate wide picture frames for a colourful postage stamp display.*

GROUPING PICTURES

A group of pictures can create a striking display that will bring a bare wall to life. Arrange pictures with perfect symmetry, or mix different shapes and sizes for a more random display.

This symmetrical arrangement of prints is bordered with two taller prints and linked together with a moiré picture bow.

Y ou can group all sorts of pictures together, provided there is some kind of link to unify the display. This might be the subject matter, as in a collection of botanical prints or landscapes, or the medium, as in a group of water-colour paintings, pencil sketches or photographs. Alternatively, the link can simply lie in the colours or tones of the pictures, or even in the way they're mounted and framed.

Try to keep the spacing between the pictures equal and to line up some of the edges for a neat finish. If one of the pictures is much larger than the others, use it as a focal point and group the other pictures around it.

A collection of pictures of the same size is best arranged with perfect symmetry in a square or rectangle, or in a neat row. To inject some order into a display of differently sized and shaped pictures, hang them inside an imaginary frame or around an imaginary cross, lining up the edges if possible.

▲ *Overhead display* *This pretty collection of floral prints is arranged in a graceful arch over the bedhead, with the smaller prints grouped around the largest one. Limed picture frames soften the overall look.*

▲ *Stencilled link* *A stencilled picture bow with trailing, tasselled ends makes these subtle, black and white prints into more of a feature, and helps to balance the arrangement. The stencil also links the prints so that they seem to belong together, although their subject matter is quite different.*

▶ *Classic collection* *A set of classical prints and relief Roman heads is displayed to perfection in this well-balanced, symmetrical arrangement. The smaller pictures are hung to each side of the two larger ones, which provide the focal point of the display.*

WALL HANGINGS

Don't hide favourite fabrics or treasured collections away from view. Display them with style on the wall to create unusual and unique wall hangings.

You can create wall hangings from all sorts of items. They needn't be expensive, but should be appealing and chosen for their shape, colour or special significance. Think of your wall hanging as a picture, allowing it the same kind of space, and make sure it works with your colour scheme and room style.

Textiles are the most obvious choice for wall hangings. Seek out intricately embroidered or ornately embellished fabric panels and brightly coloured Eastern rugs – either when you're on holiday abroad, or closer to home in ethnic shops and charity shops.

Look round your home for other ideas. You may have a collection of scarves, shawls or sarongs lying idle in a drawer, waiting for their season to come round again. Why not bring them out of hibernation and display them on the wall until you're ready to wear them? The same goes for many other accessories, including hats, evening bags and colourful beaded necklaces. All can be hung from hooks or pegs – and keeping them on view means you won't forget to wear them!

▼ *Oriental extravaganza A striking kelim rug and an Eastern embroidered panel make sumptuous wall hangings. To mount a fabric hanging, use sew-and-stick, touch-and-close fastening tape. If your hanging is heavy, avoid attaching the sticky half of the tape directly to the wall – staple it to a painted wooden batten, and mount this on the wall.*

> *Antique robe* The angular shapes and bold patterns of a Japanese kimono make a graphic wall hanging. Insert a bamboo pole or a dowel through both sleeves and spread the kimono out flat against the wall. Rest the ends of the pole on small hooks.

> *Shaker hearts* Wall hangings don't have to be large. Here, small heart-shaped sachets in checked fabrics are threaded on to a length of ribbon to make a charming country bedroom decoration.

> *Summer display* Hang your favourite straw hats and scarves on the walls of a hallway when summer is over. Here, the earthy tones of natural dyed textiles are the perfect complement for the warm colours of the straw.

> *Beaded beauty* A cherished collection of small tapestry and beaded evening bags is shown off to advantage in this glamorous wall display, perfect for a bedroom.

DECORATIVE SCREENS

When space is at a premium, freestanding screens make invaluable room dividers and clutter concealers. Decorated with imagination and flair, they can also be striking focal points.

A freestanding screen is one of the most versatile pieces of furniture you can have in your home. It can function as a temporary dividing wall – separating the sleeping area from the living space in a studio flat, for example; or as an instant cover-up for clutter at the end of the day – whether it's the children's toys or a half-finished sewing project.

A screen consists of three or four solid panels or lightweight frames, hinged together so that it can be folded flat against the wall when not needed. Although you can buy magnificent old screens from second-hand and antique furniture shops, they are often quite expensive and may need extensive restoration. A cheaper option is to buy a plain medium density fibreboard screen, available by mail order from blanks suppliers in a range of styles, and to decorate it yourself.

For a particularly luxurious finish, upholster your screen with fabric; or fit it with fabric panels if it is a frame-style screen – choosing a cloth that complements your room scheme. If it is a screen with solid panels, you could paint it or decorate it with découpage; try your hand at paint techniques such as faux finishes, stencilling, stamping or freehand designs.

▲ *Sewing screen In this tucked-away sewing corner, a cheery checked fabric has been wrapped tightly round a screen frame, with contrast pockets for sewing essentials. The solid-panel screen (inset) has been painted in soft sandy shades, then stamped with jungle-theme motifs.*

◄ Fruit découpage *A four-panel painted screen, used as a room divider in an Oriental-style flat, is an ideal showcase for imaginative decoupage – colourful fruit cutouts on a newsprint background.*

▲ Paint effects *You can use a wide range of paint techniques to decorate solid-panel screens. Here, tall, slim panels are enhanced with a dragged paint effect in pale green, and stencilled garlands running down each side.*

◄ Fourfold flowers *A large four-panel screen serves as a background for a flower-arranging corner. Fabric panels were made to fit the screen frames exactly, then attached with braid threaded through brass eyelets.*

TABLE TOP DISPLAYS

Display some favourite possessions on a table top to create a focal point in a room. It's a wonderful way of indulging your personal taste and making a corner of your home special.

▼ *The floral theme of this room is repeated in the fresh flowers, lamp base and potpourri, while the silver ornaments provide a gleaming contrast.*

The most effective table-top arrangements suit the decor of the room, so try to reflect the main colour scheme, or pick up on patterns or the theme of the room.

For a room with floral patterns you could choose a small vase of flowers and some dainty china with a sprigged pattern. A room with an Oriental theme would lend itself to a display of shiny lacquer nicknacks.

The colours you choose can either harmonize or contrast with their setting. Stark white ceramics will blend with a spacious white room, while brightly coloured pottery will add a vivid highlight.

▼ **Period piece** *This collection of 1920s and 1930s ornaments is arranged on two tables of different heights. The mirrored surfaces reflect their fascinating shapes.*

▼ **Light and airy** *The earthy tones of this display allow the rich textures of the wood and the dark animal shape to stand out against the pale background. The white sweet peas add a touch of airy lightness.*

WHAT TO DISPLAY

The display can include virtually any object – old, new, purely decorative or practical. The choice is endless, from animal miniatures, table lamps and cut glass to trinket boxes or flowers.

An effective display doesn't have to include expensive ornaments; a pretty bowl filled with colourful fruits would brighten up a simple table top in the kitchen; and a collection of glass, placed to catch light from a window, can brighten up a dark corner. The only guideline is to choose items in a range of sizes and shapes – they will be easier to arrange.

PLACING YOUR PIECES

The table top itself has an important part to play in the look – plain pine is a natural background for many textures such as brass or basket ware, and mahogany would show off silver or glass to perfection.

If the table looks better covered with a cloth, select one that suits your

display as well as your decor: lace with antique silver; sprig florals with bone china, or natural cotton with polished wood and metal ornaments.

Once you've decided where to put your display, it helps to think of the objects that you want to arrange as forming a still-life picture. Look at the dominant colours, shapes and textures and how they relate to the rest of the room. Also consider how daylight and artificial light will highlight particularly interesting features.

◀ *Paint effects* *This minimalist display in wood and china blends together because of its soft, muted colours. The amaryllis adds a lively touch.*

▼ *Oriental mood* *The rich golden tones of the cloth and curtain provide a warm setting for exotic dark ornaments. The gold tones of the furnishings also pick out the gold details on the ornaments and lamp base.*

▲ *Cottage bedroom* *The pretty china lamp base, framed picture and vase of flowers match the rest of the bedroom decor and reflect the overall country cottage feeling of the room. The scalloped tablecloth adds a charming touch.*

▼ *Kitchen still life* *A vibrant café curtain and white cloth sets the scene for a bright jug of flowers, fresh fruit and some colourful candles.*

◀Colour connection *This display shows how the flowers you choose can add something special. The intricate patterning of the blue and white china jugs is given an extra dimension by the complementary arrangement of blue and white flowers.*

▼Friendly frogs *An exhibition of a very individual taste. These endearing frogs with their different textures and colours are casually grouped, and send out an irresistible invitation for closer inspection and handling.*

▼Perfectly pink *Pale pink links the unusual flower bowls and plates with the two vases, while the black ornaments provide a welcome and dramatic contrast. The bright red tulips add a punch of colour.*

FIREPLACE FILLERS

A redundant fireplace makes an attractive display area and a useful storage space. A whole range of items – from houseplants to teddy bears – can be simultaneously shown off and neatly housed in this way.

Fireplaces are a most desirable feature in the home, providing a cosy atmosphere and a natural focal point in a room. An unused fireplace – whether permanently or just temporarily out of use – can make the perfect background for displays of all kinds, as well as a handy, easy-access storage area.

Traditional styles of fireplace, with wood or stone surrounds and generous mantelpieces and hearths, make natural display areas for flowers and plants. If you take out the grate and fireback you will have a far larger space to play with. You could use it to create an on-hand wine cellar by fitting it with wine racks – ideal for a dining room or kitchen fireplace. Smaller bedroom fireplaces can be put to use as a special home for a child's favourite teddy bears; or to house a cherished collection of Victorian dolls, perhaps.

Before you place anything in the fireplace, make sure that no soot or debris can fall down by sealing off the chimney – be sure to check with a builder first about ventilation regulations. Then line the recess with particleboard or strong cardboard, which you can paint to match the fireplace.

Cactus garden A large fireplace with a carved wooden surround makes a spectacular showcase for a cactus collection. The smallest plants run along the mantelpiece while larger specimens cluster on the tiled floor framed by the carved wood fire surround.

▶ **Summer whites** *A refreshing summer display of white daisies, pelargoniums and silvery foliage graces this original white-painted stone fireplace with elegant black cast-iron grate.*

◀ **Wine cellar** *A Victorian-style pine fire surround with a huge overmantel makes a splendid wine cellar. Line the fireplace opening and install ready-made wine racks to fill the space.*

▲ **Grate display** *A rustic display of pine cones and cinnamon bundles piled high in the grate makes a perfect temporary fireplace filler. Simply remove the display when it's time to light a fire.*

◀ **Toy store** *A nursery fireplace becomes a cosy home for a child's treasured teddies. If the fireplace is still functional, first make sure the chimney is completely sealed off and then line it with plywood or plasterboard to protect the toys from soot. If you wish, you could make a small shelf or step for the teddies to sit on.*

KITCHEN STORAGE IDEAS

*It takes no time at all to create useful storage space in
your kitchen using everyday items from garden
centres and home improvement stores.*

Whatever the size of your kitchen, extra storage space is always welcome. With a little imagination, you can turn everyday items from garden centres and home improvement stores into practical storage systems.

Garden centres stock a wide range of accessories normally associated with outdoor spaces – such as trellis panels and hanging baskets – which transplant happily to interior use. You can hang up all your saucepans and gadgets with butcher's hooks on a trellis panel cut to fit your wall space. Sand down the rough edges to make painting easier and then apply a coat of emulsion. Attach the panel to the wall securely using wall plugs. Make sure you

position the vertical slats against the wall so that the horizontal slats stand away from the wall, to allow enough space for the butcher's hooks to get a firm grip.

Ceiling-hung containers for fruits and vegetables can be made from a stack of colourful plastic colanders roped together with cord or builders' rope. Look round your local builders' merchants or do-it-yourself store for items such as lengths of rigid plastic pipe that can be glued together to make a bottle storage unit for wine or soft drinks.

When shelf space is at a premium, you can use both sides of your shelves. Screw the lids of screwtop jars firmly to the underside of a shelf, then screw on filled jars of herbs, spices and dried goods.

Storage solutions
A shopping spree in a garden centre or do-it-yourself store can provide instant kitchen storage. Hang pots and pans on a trellis, store fruit and vegetables in a colander swing, bottles in plumbing pipes or attach screwtop jars to shelves for a double-sided solution to your storage problems.

Colander swing If you have only a small refrigerator, a trio of colourful plastic colanders roped together provide space for fruit and vegetables. Slot bright orange builder's rope through the colander handles, looping twice to prevent slipping. Suspend them from a ceiling hook to provide decorative storage that swings easily out of the way.

Bottle pipes Handy filing for all sizes of bottles can be created from rigid plastic pipe found at do-it-yourself stores or left over from building work. Arrange the pipe sections to fit your space and glue together using a glue gun.

Kitchen trellis A section of garden trellis, painted to match the wall, provides instant hanging space for kitchen equipment. Cut a panel to fit your wall space, then sand and paint. Attach the trellis securely to the wall, then use butcher's hooks to hang up the pots and pans.

Shelf solution Attach a collection of screwtop jars to the underside of a shelf. Drill a hole in the centre of each lid. Position the lids on the underside of the shelf and screw up through the lids into the shelf to secure. Screw on the filled jars.

SILVER EFFECTS

Whether you go for the real thing or simply a silvery effect,
the gleaming richness of silver is cool and sophisticated.
Look for it in accessories, fabrics and even furniture.

Think silver, think cool, gleaming and elegant. Even an odd piece of silver – a teapot, sweet dish or a pair of candlesticks – adds lustrous glamour to a room.

Antique silver accessories have a beautiful matt gleam that comes from frequent use, and lots of polishing over the years. By contrast, modern silver is new and shinier and has a more up-beat, mirror-like quality.

If you want an overall silver effect in your living room, dining room or bedroom, look for fabrics and trimmings with plenty of texture – palest grey damask, moiré and silk or modern metallic fibres that gleam with silver thread. Then add silver accessories – and even furniture – that have been given an instant facelift with silver gilt or a few deft squirts of silver spray paint.

Kitchen shine Display kitchen accessories in silvery chrome and stainless steel on open shelves for an up-to-the-minute, hi-tech look.

Create silver effects in other rooms in your home. Polished chrome and steel have the appearance of silver but introduce an air of gleaming efficiency and hygiene in your kitchen and bathroom.

Silver print Use silver spray paint on plain wooden frames to make these elegant silver-effect frames. The engravings of antique silver tea and coffee pots are further enhanced by edging the mount, as here, with a line drawn with a silver pen.

Shining tableau Indian shops are a good source of silvery accessories at an affordable price. Here, silver items are grouped on a grey marble table. Fabric dotted with silver stars and an arrangement of silvery leaves and white flowers complete the look.

Dress silver Silver dressing table accessories – perfume bottles with silver tops, brushes and mirrors – arranged on a lace cloth evoke a gentle, bygone age in this traditional bedroom.

Metallic sheen Give an old chair a glamorous finish with silver spray paint. First remove the seat and strip off any old finish. Then sand down and spray with silver metallic paint. Spray paint a small side table to complete the look.

CHINA DISPLAYS

*Don't hide attractive china away in your cupboards –
put it on show around your home, to create colourful
displays – and keep it within easy reach.*

China, whether fine porcelain or
rustic earthenware, can be used
to create decorative displays
around your home. You may have a
collection of colourful ceramic plates
or odd china cups and saucers, or
perhaps an attractive dinner service
hidden away that deserves pride of
place on a sideboard or table top.

Think about how and where to
arrange your collection – shelves, a
table top, mantlepiece, windowsill or
wall all make good display surfaces.
Some china, such as a tea set or
dinner service which is in daily use,
lends itself to a formal display where
each item can be seen clearly and
accessed easily – a dresser with open

shelves is perfect for this. Heavy,
rustic-style ceramics look better in
loosely arranged, informal displays.

For the pattern and shape of plates
to be seen at their best, they need to
be displayed upright. Either use a
plastic or wooden stand, or plastic-
coated wire plate hooks for hanging
on the wall. Alternatively, a strip of
wooden beading along shelving
prevents plates from slipping.

▽ **Pride of place** *The top of a side
table or small cupboard is an ideal
spot to display a handsome collection of
china, such as the Victorian-style jugs
and pitchers shown below, or traditional
blue and white china (right).*

> **Simply nostalgic** *A collection of floral-patterned Victorian china makes a delightful corner display. You can create a display like this out of very few pieces – one or two jugs and some odd cups and saucers have been used here to charming effect. A background of patterned ceramic tiles against the walls creates the perfect foil for the china.*

◀ **Plate rack** *A display of china plates on a wooden dresser is given a fresh, up-to-the-minute feel by the clever combination of modern Mediterranean colours. Seashells along the shelf edges complete the seaside atmosphere.*

▲ **Colour brights** *Brightly coloured ceramic jugs decorated with lively contemporary designs make a striking display on a kitchen dresser. The jugs have been placed almost randomly on the shelves to give the kitchen an informal, relaxed feel.*

◀ **Lid art** *Junk shops and garage sales are the perfect sources for odd pieces of china. You can create a distinctive display from almost anything, as this lively collection of serving dish lids demonstrates. Classic and oriental-design lids in various shapes and sizes have been used in this simple but effective wall arrangement.*

DISPLAYING GLASS CONTAINERS

*Glass containers come in all shapes, sizes, colours
and textures. Display them creatively and a dull corner
can be brightened in an instant.*

Bring your glassware out of the cupboard and try arranging it by colour, by function, or in an eye-catching mix of colours, textures and shapes. You don't need a large or special collection – simply grouping two glass vases together is the start of an attractive display.

Light brings out the colour and sparkle of glass, so when arranging your display, place it where it will pick up either natural or artificial light. Backlighting from a window is a simple but very effective source of light; overhead lighting in an alcove can also work well, or you could place nightlights inside glass containers for a romantic glow.

The surface where you display your glass containers will be led by the type of glass in your collection, but a glass or mirrored base maximizes the lighting effects.

Whatever your collection you will make the most of your display by keeping the glass sparkling clean.

Window dressing *Glass shelves across an uncurtained window make an excellent setting for a display of clear, coloured glass. The glass containers create a partial screen while allowing plenty of light into the room.*

84

From the kitchen *Victorian jelly moulds and old glass bottles can be simply arranged on wooden shelves for a charming country look. A wooden dresser would be an attractive alternative for this type of glass display.*

Creative colour *A vibrant collection of opaque, coloured glassware makes a stunning focal point in this deep window recess.*

Frosties *Two carefully placed containers can make an effective display. Frosted glass vases in pretty pastels are eye-catching when placed against neutral, textured surfaces.*

Sitting pretty *A dressing table makes the perfect background for a collection of perfume bottles. The highly polished wood accentuates the reflective qualities of the glass.*

Seashore Ideas

*Whether you choose copies or the real thing, the familiar
shapes of seashore motifs will dress up your bathroom
and remind you of happy summer days by the sea.*

The seashore can provide all
kinds of ideas for effective
decorating, from a handful
of shells adorning a mirror to a
whole theme for a room. Familiar
seashore objects – shells, fish,
boats – and cool seaside colours
instantly conjure up happy memories
of lazy summer days by the sea.

Seashore motifs are a popular choice for bathrooms but you can use them anywhere in your home.
Look for them on fabrics, tiles, wallpaper borders and on
fresh-looking accessories such as soap dishes, light pulls
and shower curtain hooks.

The distinctive graphic outlines of seashore motifs,
which have become such a popular decorating choice,
make excellent motifs for stamping or stencilling projects.
They are simple to reproduce and make pleasing designs.

▲ ***Beneath the waves*** *Wavy shelf trims fixed to the
side of the bath and on a narrow ledge installed at
chair rail height give an immediate underwater feel to
this cool, blue and green seaside bathroom. Shells,
small fish and scattered starfish add to the theme.*

Although shells remain firm favourites, pebbles,
pieces of driftwood and even seaglass – fragments
of coloured glass washed smooth
by the sea – can all be used for
accessories. Try gluing pebbles
or small pieces of driftwood to
chest or cupboard door
handles with epoxy resin or a
glue gun. Or fill a glass jar
with sea glass, and set it
on a window ledge to
catch the light.

▶ *Seeing starfish* Paint a cascade of assorted starfish in bright pastels, then glue them with epoxy resin or a glue gun to cupboard doors. Real starfish are becoming scarce so you could buy or make your own plaster copies.

▲ *Tropical bathing* Shell-printed coral curtains and a coral wave border stencil set the scene in this inviting seashore bathroom. The room is enhanced with exotic fish accessories and a windowsill shell display. The end of the bath is an ideal place for showing off your seashore accessories.

▲ *Seahorse style* A delightful brass seahorse makes a fine hook for a shower curtain tieback. Use natural cord or rope for the tieback to emphasize the look.

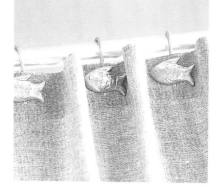

▲ *Fish clips* Small metal fish attached to clips swim lazily along the top of a shower curtain. Look for novelty clips in bath or curtain accessories shops or you could use children's toy fish.

▶ *Shell chic* Scallop shells are the dominant image on this painted cupboard. First, paint the shells to match or contrast with the background, or leave them natural, if preferred. Then stick the shells or plaster copies to your chosen piece of furniture.

FERN DETAILS

Enjoy the appeal of fresh greenery and the spirit of springtime by introducing fern details into your home – as a motif on walls, fabrics and accessories, or with natural displays of the genuine article.

The Victorians had a love affair with ferns and filled their conservatories with them. Their delicate leaf shapes and the freshness of a palette of pale greens brought light and air into stuffy parlours. The same is true today. Make use of these evocative plants – whether fresh or artificial – and you can bring an instant feeling of springtime to your home.

Ferns are a longstanding favourite motif of furnishing fabric and accessory designers. Look for them printed on upholstery and curtain fabrics; painted on wood and china; and etched into glassware. You'll also find fern motifs woven into towels and linens – they're an especially popular choice for the bathroom and bedroom, where they help create a fresh and airy atmosphere.

You can easily create your own fern designs. Buy a fern stamp or stencil – or use the real thing – and apply an all-over fern pattern, or just a delicate border, to your walls. You can use the stamp or stencil with fabric paint to create matching cushions or bedlinen. Set off the results with a display of real potted ferns.

▼ **Bathroom ferns** *Ferns are favourites for the bathroom. Here, a painted shelf bears a collection of fern-themed accessories, from towels and pots to linen bags. The wall has also been decorated using fresh fern fronds as templates. Press the fronds flat, coat them on one side with emulsion/latex paint and press on to the wall. Lay clean paper over the fern and use a small sponge roller to transfer the pattern.*

Botanical prints With their delicate colouring and distinctive outlines, ferns make excellent prints. A grouping of two or three would look pretty in a hallway or a study. You can find fern prints ready-framed or to frame yourself in print shops and second-hand book shops.

Natural combination A feathery fern motif adorns the cream centre panel of this cushion. The border of natural hopsack creates a soft frame for the image. You can create similar effects on ready-made cushion covers using fabric paints and a fern stamp or stencil.

Fern collection This attractive grouping of potted ferns shows the variety of shades and delicate leaf shapes to be found. The twig wreath on the wall and folk art bird add a touch of whimsy to the charming conservatory table.

For town and country Although fern motifs suggest a relaxed country look, this sofa upholstered in a smart fern print proves that they can be equally at home in more sophisticated room schemes, adding welcome freshness.

Leaf Details

The simple shapes of leaves provide a stylish design detail that will add a refreshing natural touch to your home. Introduce them in printed form on fabrics and wallcoverings – or use the real thing.

Leaves provide nature's most enduring design motifs. Their graphic outlines are instantly recognizable and are popular with fabric and wallcovering designers. Curtains, upholstery and carpets often bear a stylized leaf motif, and leaf designs on wallcoverings never go out of fashion.

You can capture the spirit of nature with a few deftly placed leaf motifs scattered around your home. Try cutting out simple leaf shapes from green fabric and bonding them on to cushions or throws. Or create an attractive display by pressing or preserving leaves in glycerine, then framing them and grouping them together on the wall. You could also incorporate them into wreaths and dried flower arrangements. Strong evergreens such as ivy or laurel leaves can be sprayed silver or gold for an instant party table decoration.

▼ *Pressed leaves*
A handful of leaves collected on a country walk has been pressed flat then coated with white spray paint to make unique leaf decorations. Silver or gold paint could also be used to make Christmas leaf displays.

Golden clips Add a glamorous leafy touch to curtains with these gold metallic leaf clips, available in home furnishings departments.

Leafy throw Give a simple fringed throw a spring-fresh look with scattered leaves. Cut basic leaf shapes from plain green fabric and attach them to the throw with a few deft stitches. For a no-sew alternative, you could bond the leaves to the fabric with fusible webbing.

Party glasses Use fine ribbon to tie small, artificial gold leaves to the stems of wine glasses for a stylish party table. You could spray real leaves such as ivy with gold paint to create a similar effect.

Designer detail Distinctively shaped oak leaves, their rich autumn colours preserved in glycerine, can be used in a variety of dried arrangements. Use them to decorate accessories such as the simple muslin-wrapped twig wreath and picture frame shown here.

IMPROMPTU FLOWER ARRANGEMENTS

*When a formal vase seems too grand, arrange flowers in an
unusual container. For sheer simplicity, stick to a single type
of flower in each impromptu arrangement.*

You can turn practically any watertight container into an instant vase – a teacup, an eggcup, a candlestick or even an empty tin can. Just add water, pop in a couple of flowers, and you have an attractive instant display.

Stop and think before you throw out a jar or tin – it could have a new lease of life as a vase. Wash it out, soak off any labels and smooth off any rough edges with abrasive paper.

Keep a look out for other unusual containers to recycle. For example, an old soft drink bottle can make a perfect container for long-stemmed flowers such as anemones or roses, and a single sherry glass will set off the small, delicate blooms of violets or forget-me-nots.

You can transform everyday objects with a quick flourish – try knotting a brightly coloured scrap of cord or ribbon round the top of a milk bottle, then pop in a single daffodil or tulip.

Cup of blooms
*An eggcup
makes a charming
instant container
for small blooms
such as these ixora.*

Perfect posies
*A glass candlestick
and miniature coffee
cup make elegant
containers for tiny
posies of primulas. Fill
the containers with
water, cut all the
flower stems to the
same length, then
place them in the
water. Tie a swirl of
sheer ribbon round the
stem of the candlestick
for a final delicate
flourish.*

> **Summer delight** *A double display doubles the impact. For a fresh summer arrangement, make up twin bunches of garden flowers – nasturtiums were used here – put them in identical sundae glasses and place them together for an attractive display.*

▲ **Alternative chic** *Pure white ranunculus mingled with sprigs of fragrant rosemary elevate empty tin cans to designer status. Clean out the tins and soak off their labels then smooth any rough edges with abrasive paper and buff them to a fine shine. Tie a twisted cord of raffia around the cans, then simply fill them with water and flowers.*

▲ **Container elegance** *Outsize glass tumblers or jars become showcases for straight-stemmed roses, their slender stems and pastel-coloured blooms protected behind the clear glass walls. Strip off the leaves so the water does not discolour, then cut the stems so the flowers stand well below the rim.*

KITCHEN CONTAINERS

Give silver and aluminium colanders, moulds, cake tins and even watering cans a new role to play – cleaned and polished up and displayed on a shelf or table, they make stylish pots and vases for plants, fragrant herbs and cut flowers.

Gleaming brioche moulds hold tiny sage, rosemary and thyme plants and there's bay, fennel and thyme in the giant colander.

With their shiny surfaces and simple shapes, silvery and aluminium containers are the perfect contrast for the intricate forms of many plants and flowers.

Water-tight containers, such as ice-buckets, metal bowls and moulds, make instant vases. You can use them for temporary displays of plants as well, but they are unsuitable for long-term use as they lack drainage.

Colanders have plenty of drainage, so they're ideal for displaying plants. After you've watered the plants, leave the colanders to drain through before putting them in position.

If you are using your kitchen container for pot plants, either keep the plants in their plastic pots or gently remove them and pack them into the container with damp potting compost. Outdoor plants shouldn't be kept indoors for too long, so put them back outside after a few weeks.

Make sure your kitchen container is really clean and has a smooth base so that it won't scratch precious furniture. If the base feels rough, you could place the container on a pretty cloth or doiley. Alternatively, rest the container on a couple of pieces of kitchen paper, folding in the edges of the paper so they won't show.

DAISY GARDEN

Create a stylish indoor garden with cut shasta daisies, or if you can't get these, use white chrysanthemums.

MATERIALS

Shasta daisies

Bun moss

Two soaked florists' foam blocks

Old newspaper

Two cake tins

Watering can

Scissors

1 PREPARING THE CAKE TINS
Cut two blocks of florists' foam long enough to fit across each cake tin, and deep enough to reach just below the rim. Place the foam in the tins. Then fill in the sides with smaller pieces of florists' foam.

2 PREPARING THE WATERING CAN
Crumple up the newspaper and pack it tightly into the bottom half of the watering can. Rest a large piece of florists' foam on the newspaper so that it reaches just below the rim of the can, adjusting the newspaper if necessary. Pack in the foam block with more crumpled newspaper.

3 ADDING THE FLOWERS
Trim the daisies so the stems are about 15-20cm (6-8in) long. Strip the leaves off the bottom 2.5cm (1in) of the stems only. Push the stems 2.5cm (1in) into the foam blocks, singly and in twos and threes, arranging them at different angles for a natural look.

4 ADDING THE MOSS
Pack the moss tightly over the surface of the foam to create a dense, velvety effect. Keep the display in a cool, bright spot.

An infrequently used ice-bucket is turned into an impromptu vase. This ice-bucket is filled with tulips, daffodils and bright yellow Turk's-cap ranunculus. The leaves were kept on the tulips to provide a green foil for the brighter colours of the flowers and to add bulk to the display.

VASE IDEAS

*Arranging flowers in creative containers can be time
consuming, but when you have the right vase for your blooms,
you can create beautiful arrangements in a few minutes.*

You can arrange flowers in anything that will hold water, from a tank vase to a teapot, but it is much easier if you have the correct size vase. Having the right container also gives you confidence if you are unsure of your flower arranging skills, as the flowers will naturally fall into a pleasing display.

Collect a few specially designed vases in different sizes so you are ready for any unexpected bunches of flowers. Glass or china vases with wide tops and narrower middles hold the stems in a firm bunch while allowing the flowers to fan out and arrange themselves. Others have narrow tops and wide bases and are designed to hold a few blooms, but still allow them plenty of water.

Bowls are an excellent choice for low arrangements, but place florists'

Glass display A tall green glass vase is a harmonious choice for this country arrangement of green arum lilies, buds and evergreens, while the cheery frosted glass jugs (below) complement these bright sunflowers.

foam or crumpled chicken wire inside to support the flower heads. Hold the foam or wire in place with florists' tape. Flowers arranged in bowls should be cut short so that the finished effect is of a rounded cushion of blooms with no stems visible.

Modern glass tank vases are very useful as they allow you to create high impact displays with little effort. For the most dramatic effect, confine the flowers to a single variety but use masses of them. It is also useful to have one or two tiny pots or bud vases for single stems or small flowers.

Bowl harmony *A low bowl works well when filled with short-stemmed blooms. Place florists' foam or crumpled chicken wire in the bottom of the bowl to support the flowers, cutting the stems short to create a closely packed, rounded display that complements the shape of the bowl.*

Rustic style *Tulip stems can look floppy if not supported. One solution is to put them in a vase that comes high up the stems, yet doesn't restrict their free-form style. Here, tulips are packed into a stoneware container which echoes the graceful oval shapes of the flower heads.*

Spring tanks *Glass tank vases are ideal for instant flower arranging. Here, tall tanks support rigid blooms, such as daffodils, and floppy grass stems, while tulips and anemones are perfectly balanced in chunky glass containers with rounded interiors.*

Victorian trio *A set of tall china vases, reminiscent of Victorian times, is set off to perfection when filled with a softly pretty arrangement of creamy, long-stemmed wild flowers.*

TERRACOTTA STYLE

Decorate terracotta flower pots to draw attention to favourite plants and to brighten up your home. There are lots of simple ideas to choose from – try tying the pot with a casual ribbon bow, or painting it or covering it with fabric.

▼ *These lively terracotta pots have been covered in bold floral fabrics, glued in place with PVA, then varnished with a thinned solution of PVA.*

There are lots of ways to decorate plain terracotta pots. You can cover them with fabric, stencil on motifs, paint them with bright, solid bands of colour or use a subtle paint effect, such as sponging, or simply tie them with crêpe paper ribbon or natural raffia.

If you know which plants the pot will contain, bear them in mind when you plan the decorations. For example, if you have some dainty grey and silvery green herbs, paint the pots in soft, subtle shades, using a broken colour effect, such as colourwashing, or stencil on a fine foliage motif. Likewise, if you have a collection of cacti, paint the pots in bold, colourful, geometric patterns with a Mexican feel or wrap them in bright fabric.

Before you decorate your pot, make sure that the surface is clean. If the pot is unglazed and will be used indoors, paint it with matt or silk vinyl emulsion or acrylic paint. If the pot is to go outside, use masonry paint, which is very hardwearing; you can buy masonry paint from decorating merchants. Use special ceramic paints for glazed pots.

▼ *Even the simplest decorative touch can make a terracotta pot into a stylish showpiece. Here, a cream coloured, crêpe paper ribbon has been tied into an exuberant bow around the rim of the pot, and its knot has been threaded with wheat. It sets off the natural display of dried cereals to perfection.*

▼ *These terracotta pots have been stencilled with seashore motifs, then decorated with small dots and neat borders around the rims. Only one colour of paint has been used, which shows that a design doesn't have to be very complicated to be effective.*

The neat rim borders were achieved using masking tape, while the dots were painted on free-hand with a fine artists' brush. White masonry paint was used because it is very hardwearing, so the pots can be displayed outside throughout the summer.

◀ *Geometric, Mexican style designs in riotous bright colours cover these cacti pots, enhancing the plants' dramatic shapes. Copy this look using bright acrylic paints.*

PAINTING POTS

One of the most striking ways to decorate terracotta pots is to paint them. Even a simple, all-over wash of colour can transform a pot, especially if you add texture by applying the paint with a sponge or stippling brush.

Striped effects and sleek geometric patterns are easy to achieve using masking tape. Just mask off the surface on each side of the area you want to paint, let the paint dry, then carefully remove the tape. Repeat this process to build up your design. Use a small decorators' brush to apply the paint, and a fine artists' brush to add detailing. Alternatively, stencil motifs on to the painted background, using a stencil brush or a sponge.

Coloured Baskets

Bright baskets, painted or dyed a cheerful colour, retain all the traditional qualities of basketware but look a little more special. Choose or paint one in a colour to complement your home.

▼ *A brilliant blue basket is cleverly paired with a display of grape hyacinths. If you are using your painted baskets for a planted display, put another container inside the basket, or line it with plastic.*

Natural cane wicker baskets have charm, but the smartest baskets of all are coloured – painted bright, rich primary shades or dyed in subtle hues. The choice of colour depends on the room: a bright red shopping basket filled with fruit adds cheer to a kitchen, while a small basket, painted soft pink and filled with guest soaps, adds a welcoming touch to a bathroom.

Most shops that sell natural baskets also stock painted or dyed ones, but it is perfectly easy and much more fun to paint one yourself. In fact, it is an ideal way to resurrect an old basket, or make an inexpensive one look special. For rich matt colours, use two coats of emulsion/latex, or experiment with aerosol paints. For more subtle colours, brush or rub on artists' inks.

◀ *The rich plum shades of this colour-stained basket are echoed in the abundant display of lilac and heather. Reproduce the colour effect on this basket by rubbing artists' inks into the weave of an unvarnished, pale wicker basket. Use two different colours of undiluted ink and with a soft cloth, rub each colour separately into the basket, letting them merge. For a basket of this size you need one bottle of each colour.*

◀ *Dazzling golds and greens form the perfect Christmas table centre-piece. The basket and leaves can be sprayed at the same time – place them on newspaper and work in a well ventilated room. Take care to follow the instructions on the can to prevent the nozzle from clogging with paint.*

VALENTINE BASKET

This little basket, filled with heart-shaped chocolates, makes a perfect gift for Valentine's day. Originally a pale wicker colour, it was painted with a couple of coats of household latex paint. Once the paint had dried, the sides were stencilled with rich red hearts.

To stencil the basket, make a template by cutting out your chosen motif from a piece of thick paper. Hold the template firmly on the basket, then use a sponge to apply the paint over the stencil shape.

FLORAL IMPACT

Flowers that are bold in shape and strong in colour lend themselves to dramatic arrangements. You need buy only a few flowers, careful selection will ensure maximum impact.

Massed colour is the key to success when you want to create a striking floral arrangement. The flowers don't have to be expensive and if they are large you only need a few. 'Architectural' flowers, such as lilies, sunflowers or gladioli, are dramatic enough by themselves and don't need other flowers or foliage. If your chosen blooms are small, use lots of them and confine your choice to one or two colours that work well together. A vase of mixed flowers looks very pretty but doesn't have the show-stopping effect that a mass of strong colour has.

For the best effect, coordinate your vase or container with the flowers. A brightly coloured arrangement with a matching or boldly contrasting vase can be stunning for the adventurous.

For high impact displays, it is important to have enough space to show off the flowers. To make an effective summer arrangement, use two or three spikes of delphiniums or lupins and put them in a tall

▲ *Orange impact A mix of Oriental and Calla lilies in warm orange tones makes a bold statement in an old terracotta urn. The small earthenware pot of bright orange ranunculus nestled at the base adds to the impact.*

container in a fireplace. Or try a row of matching narrow glass containers, each holding a single bloom, on a mantelpiece. You could place a dramatic arrangement at the end of a narrow hall, or in a bay window, which provides a natural display area.

▷ **Loud trumpets** *Clay pots of red and white amaryllis, with their blooms at the peak of perfection, are grouped together on a butler's tray for maximum effect. The bold contrasts of red and lime green help the impact. The flowerpots have been wrapped in coloured paper to match the room scheme.*

◁ **Group show** *Just two varieties of spring flowers – tulips and hyacinths – are displayed here in a collection of mixed glass containers that are linked by their single colour. The result is a most effective contemporary-style grouping.*

▷ **Reverse impact** *If your paintwork and soft furnishings are vibrant, brightly coloured flowers would fight for position. Instead, choose pale shades, such as the delicate pink peonies set here against a deep turquoise background. The flowers are equally eye-catching but achieve the right balance.*

▲ **Shimmering white** *This cool, contemporary collection of white flowers in white and silver containers proves that you don't have to have bright colours to achieve high impact. The all-white surroundings and massed white flowers create a fresh, modern look.*

GREENERY DISPLAYS

*Green, nature's most soothing colour, is all around us in a
wealth of shades. Use plants and foliage to create striking
displays in your home at a fraction of the cost of fresh flowers.*

ouseplants of all varieties introduce
natural touches of green to your
home, but for a different effect try
creating displays from cut greenery; it is
equally effective and, unlike houseplants,
doesn't require long-term care.

Select leaves in shapes and shades to
complement each other. Silvery green euca-
lyptus comes in several varieties which look
very effective when used together, or you
could add other silvery leaves such as
lambs' ears and helichrysum. Mix yellow
greens with dark greens, variegated leaves
with plain, and add the odd creamy or
green-tinted flower to lighten the effect.
Unusual green spring flowers such as helle-
bores and bells of Ireland look quite superb
in green displays.

Simple, sturdy containers work best with

*Buckets of green A mixture of dark,
glossy evergreens and green
flowers has been used for this sunlit,
leafy display. By contrast, silvery
leaves and small creamy yellow
tulips (inset) create a cool and
refreshing touch.*

greenery and enhance the simplicity of
the display. Galvanized, cone-shaped flower
buckets are excellent because they support
large branches without tipping over, but
similar metal buckets or heavy stone or glass
jars would work just as well. In a large space,
group the containers together – in a fireplace, for instance – or stand them on the
floor in a hallway. Cluster small plants in
unusual pots and brighten dark corners with
masses of refreshing green.

▼ **Watery greens** *Create an unusual but effective display of small plants and bulbs by placing them in glass jars and vases filled with water. Small plants float on the water, others are anchored to a base of pebbles while the graceful arches of amaryllis leaves and beargrass frame the scene.*

▶ **Step by step** *Stairs or a flight of steps, provided they are light and wide enough for safety, can make a natural display area for a collection of houseplants. Here, a white-painted, cottage-style staircase provides the perfect foil for a variety of green houseplants.*

▶ **Mossy trees** *Make an instant mini topiary using moss, a florists' foam ball and intertwined branches for the 'trunk'. Insert the branches into the foam ball and attach fresh sphagnum moss to it using craft glue and florists' pins. Spray the tree at intervals with water to keep it fresh.*

◀ **Shelf greenery** *Tiny houseplants look most effective when displayed together. Here, an old corner cupboard makes a delightful background for an arrangement of plant-filled coffee cups and little jugs.*

IVY LEAGUE

Twist and tease trailing stems of potted ivy up and around simple frames of twigs or wire. Ivy is really easy to look after and will continue to climb happily around the frame to give you a long-lasting ornamental display.

▼ *Deep green ivy plants, set into terracotta flower pots, clamber up a rustic twig cone and a metal frame, cleverly made from an old coat hanger.*

Take a fresh look at the humble ivy – so often just used as a foil for other household plants – and give it centre stage with a simple frame to twist and twine around. The effect is classic, whether the frame is rustic or modern, and it will look effective in any room in the home.

CHOOSING IVY

Ivy comes in a range of types and sizes, from small-leaved, variegated varieties to large, deep, glossy green types. Ivy cuttings root very easily – the best time to raid your garden or patio is in the autumn. Alternatively, you can buy small ivy plants very cheaply from most garden centres, florists and many large supermarkets.

MAKING FRAMES

Ivy is perfect for training up and around a frame. It grows rapidly and attaches itself by aerial roots to almost any support. Large garden centres may sell ornamental frames particularly for this purpose, but it's much more fun and economical to make your own.

The quickest frames are made from twigs taken from the garden or a forest walk. It's best to use ones that still have a little sap left in them. Very old, dead twigs will snap and break if you try to bend them into shape.

Alternatively, make a simple shape from a wire coat hanger. You don't need wire cutters or pliers. Simply pull the hanger into a diamond or circular shape with your hands.

Commercial wire frames, like this dramatic spiral, are sold in large garden centres. Once the ivy is established, keep it trimmed to ensure that the shape of the frame is still visible.

SHAPED IVY DISPLAY

You can assemble this lovely pot of stylised ivy really quickly, and with just a few ingredients. No special gardening skills are required.

Buy ivy plants with long tendrils so that you can create the shape instantly. The plant will fill out and continue to grow around the frame over the coming weeks, until the wire is completely covered. Alternatively, take cuttings from ivy growing in your garden, as described above.

1 PREPARING THE POTS
Spread out some newspaper on your work surface and gently ease the ivy plants out of their pots. Keep the root balls and compost intact. Put a little soil in the bottom of the large pot so that the ivy will sit level with the rim of the pot.

2 PLANTING THE IVY
Plant the ivy in the large pot. If you think the ivy is too bulky, gently divide it by teasing the roots apart. Make sure you retain the pieces with the longest stems.

For a more rustic look, use three twigs to make a frame like a wigwam. Simply place the twigs around the edge of the pot and tie them together at the top with florists' or strong fuse wire.

MATERIALS

Two medium-size ivy plants

Some extra soil or compost

Plant pot (plastic or terracotta) about 14cm (5½in) deep

Newspaper

Metal coathanger

Moss (optional)

3 MAKING THE FRAME
Squeeze the coat hanger hook into a V shape and press it into the soil in the centre of the pot. Take care not to damage the ivy roots. Pull the coat hanger into a pleasing shape.

4 TRAINING THE IVY
Twist the longest stems of ivy together and twine them up the metal frame. Twist on the shorter stems.

DRIED FLOWER SWAG

This swag of pretty dried flowers will help to brighten up a dull corner. Try hanging it over a mantelpiece, above a bedhead or on a kitchen dresser. With its rich colours it will make a beautiful natural decoration for your home.

▼ *Bring nature into your home with this long-lasting dried flower swag. All the materials are readily available so it won't cost much to make.*

This dried flower swag may look elaborate, but it's really very simple to make. It's economical too, and all the ingredients are widely available for most of the year.

You can use flowers you've dried yourself or buy them ready-dried. Dried flowers can be obtained from many different outlets, such as department stores, craft shops and gift shops. Alternatively, you can buy them from mail order suppliers.

MATERIALS

Bunch of yellow achillea

Bunch of green achillea

Bunch of white or bleached achillea

Bunch of bleached broom flowers

Bunch of open carthamus

Bunch of wired gold and rust helichrysum

Bunch of natural lagurus or any fluffy cream-coloured seedheads

1.5m (1⅝yd) of 22mm (1in) wide double-sided green satin ribbon

6.4m (7yd) of florists' wire

4m (4½yd) of plastic-coated garden wire

Your dried flower swag will last indefinitely. Trim the ends with toning ribbon bows for a pretty finishing touch.

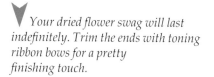

1 MAKING HELICHRYSUM BUNCHES
Make a small bunch of green achillea, a few sprigs of broom, two heads of helichrysum and three heads of lagurus. Cut a 46cm (18in) length of florists' wire and bind it tightly around the stems just below the flowerheads, wrapping the wire around three or four times. Trim the ends of the wire. Make a total of seven bunches in this way.

2 MAKING CARTHAMUS BUNCHES
Make a small bunch of yellow achillea, white achillea and two heads of open carthamus. Cut a 46cm (18in) length of florists' wire and bind it tightly around the stems, just below the flowerheads, wrapping the wire around three or four times. Trim the ends of the wire. Trim the stems to 7.5-10cm (3-4in). Make a total of seven bunches like this.

3 STARTING THE SWAG
Make a large loop at one end of the garden wire. This will be used to hang the swag. Take a helichrysum bunch and hold it in your hand with the wire loop. Using the same length of garden wire bind the loop and the flowers together tightly, wrapping the wire around three or four times.

4 BUILDING UP THE SWAG
Take a carthamus bunch and lay it over the first bunch to cover the stems. Bind it tightly in place with the garden wire. Continue like this, alternating the helichrysum and carthamus bunches of flowers until you have only one bunch left.

5 COMPLETING THE SWAG
Lay the last bunch in the opposite direction to the other bunches. Make a loop behind it with the garden wire and then bind the garden wire tightly around the bunch of flowers and the loop. If necessary, adjust the positioning of the flowers to hide the join of the last bunch. Tie a ribbon bow on to the loops at each end.

MINI FLOWER RINGS

Decorate mini wicker rings with paper, silk or dried flowers and foliage, and hang them from pretty paper ribbons to create attractive wall decorations or gifts for friends. The wreaths take only a few minutes to make.

Paper roses and leaves, dried achillea and glixia, and satin ribbon bows adorn these pretty wicker rings, hung on a raffia paper ribbon.

These pretty deco-rated wicker rings are just as much fun to create as larger, more elaborate wreaths. Because they're so small, they're quick and inexpensive to make and you can turn out several in an afternoon.

You'll find small circular and oval wicker rings in craft shops, gift shops and department stores. Shops like these also sell dried, paper and silk flowers.

For the finishing touch, you'll need wide ribbon in a shade which tones with the flowers and leaves. Raf-fia and paper ribbon are a good choice and you can buy these in florists and craft shops.

This pretty wicker ring is decorated with silk flowers in soft shades of pink and white against deep russet fern leaves. If you prefer a blue and white scheme, use white daisies, white rosebuds, blue cornflowers and green ferns instead

MATERIALS

Wicker ring, 13cm (5in) in diameter

Glue gun or tube of strong, quick-drying glue

Three white fabric lilies

Three small pale pink fabric roses

8-12 small pale and dark pink fabric flowers

Four short fronds of bracken, preserved with glycerine or dried

1m (1yd) of 4cm (1½in) wide paper ribbon

Matching thread and scissors

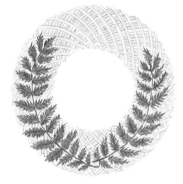

1 GLUEING ON THE BRACKEN
Using a glue gun or quick-drying glue, stick a bracken frond on each side of the ring so that the stems meet at the base. Allow the glue to dry.

▼ *Twine fake ivy round a wicker ring and slip in a cluster of fake berries to make this instant wreath.*

2 ADDING THE SMALL FLOWERS
Starting just below the top of one of the pieces of bracken, and working downwards, glue the small flowers to the bracken, finishing with a rose. Repeat on the other side, keeping the arrangement symmetrical.

3 ADDING THE LILIES
Glue on the lilies in a tight triangle at the bottom centre of the wreath. Then add the remaining rose, small flowers and ferns.

4 ADDING THE RIBBON
Cut a 50cm (20in) length of ribbon. At one end, fold under 9cm (3½in) and glue it down to form a loop. Glue the ribbon to the back of the decorated wicker ring with the loop at the top and the 'tail' extending about 12cm (4½in) below the base of the ring. Cut the base end of the ribbon to form a neat V-shape.

5 MAKING THE BOW
Cut a 40cm (16cm) length of ribbon and tie it in a neat bow. Trim each bow tail into a V-shape. Using matching thread, tie the bow to the ribbon trim at the bottom of the loop.

WAYS WITH POTPOURRI

Potpourri provides an attractive way of adding a subtle hint of fragrance to your home. It acts as a natural air freshener and its cheerful colours can brighten any room.

Potpourri not only smells good but it looks marvellous too. As well as the traditional mixtures of dried flower petals, there are blends containing large flower heads, seeds, twigs, wood shavings, nuts and even dried fruit. In their natural state, the ingredients of potpourri come in warm, rather muted shades but you can also find more vibrant mixes that have been stained with dyes.

Heap these heady mixtures into ornamental bowls or baskets and place them on display to perfume the air. Choose the container to suit both the potpourri and the style of the room. A seashell heaped with lavender and larkspur is just right for a bathroom, while a wooden bowl packed with spicy, scented pine cones adds a welcome fragrance in a cloakroom or hall.

Circles of flowers An ornamental dish, lined with a swirl of moiré fabric provides the container for an old-fashioned, rose-petal potpourri. Decorate the rim of the dish with large blooms and flower sprays that complement the colours of the fabric and the potpourri.

Clever displays *Add colour to a display of ornaments with one or two small bowls piled high with potpourri. The container can be plain or decorative and made from almost any material – so long as it fits in with the other ornaments and the decoration of the room.*

Perfumed gifts *Potpourri makes a perfect present for almost any occasion. Here a child's fortune game, made from coloured origami paper, provides the container for tiny, scented flower petals. Wrap the container in a square of silky fabric and tie with sheer ribbon.*

Wall flowers *Use a flexible embroidery hoop to make this delicate potpourri wall hanging. Cut a circle of cardboard the same size as the hoop, and two circles of fine net 5cm (2in) larger all round than the hoop. Stitch a lace trim round the edge of one of the net circles. Lay the untrimmed net circle and then the cardboard over the outer ring of the hoop. Spread potpourri over the cardboard then place the trimmed net on top and close the hoop tightly with the second ring so that the lace trim is outside the hoop. Trim with ribbon bows and roses, then hang on the wall.*

Scented sachets *Tiny bags made from net or lace and filled with potpourri create sweet-scented pockets around your home. Fold a rectangle of fine net in half and stitch the side edges with narrow self-neatening seams. Add a lace trim round the top edge, fill with a handful of potpourri and fasten the neck of the bag with a rubber band. Tie a length of ribbon over the rubber band and use it to hang the sachet from a bedstead or chair back*

POTPOURRI BASKETS

Miniature baskets are ideal for displaying your favourite potpourri – the open weave ensures that the perfume will fill the whole room. For a charming finish, trim the front of the basket with a tiny cluster of flowers to match the potpourri.

Rose potpourri calls for a rose trim: here, a small bunch of rose heads and lavender grace the front of this round basket. They were simply glued in place.

Decorating baskets with dried flowers is quick, easy and a great way of using up material left over from larger displays. If you need to buy the flowers, look out for individual flower heads or small, budget-priced bouquets which are available from many florists and supermarkets. Small baskets are sold in craft stores and bargain shops.

The trim doesn't have to be entirely floral – complement the contents of the basket by adding an additional trim, such as acorns or tiny cones.

LAVENDER AND ROSES

You can make this miniature potpourri basket in less than half an hour – the floral trim is just glued in place. If you are buying the glue especially, choose a small tube with a fine nozzle so that it's easier to apply the glue accurately. If you do make a mistake and have to pull off your trim, don't worry; multi-purpose glue is fairly easy to peel off, and shouldn't damage the surface if you are careful.

MATERIALS

Four rose heads plus leaves

Three stems of dried lavender

Matching pot pourri

Small basket

Multi-purpose glue

Sticky tape

1 GLUEING THE ROSES Arrange the rose heads and the smaller leaves in an attractive pattern on the side of the basket. Stick each piece firmly in place with glue. You may need to hold the rose heads in place for a few seconds while the glue takes hold.

2 ADDING THE LAVENDER
Bind together two or three short stems of lavender with a small length of sticky tape, then glue them to the basket just below the rose heads.

3 COMPLETING THE BASKET
Glue on a couple of larger leaves to hide the sticky tape on the lavender. Fill the basket with the potpourri.

Shiny bath pearls can be stuck to the basket with glue or double-sided sticky tape. They can be peeled off quite easily later. This aqua coloured basket, painted with household latex paint, is filled with reindeer moss and scattered with tiny sneezewort flowers and pretty shell soaps.

HIDDEN LINING

If you are filling a large basket, line it with clear polythene to stop flakes of potpourri or moss falling through the weave.

Red and purple soaps and bath pearls nestle in vibrant potpourri. Small sprigs of lavender are tied to the handle with wired burgundy ribbon to complement the colours of the basket's contents.

FLOATING FLOWERS

You can create a striking floral arrangement in a few seconds by snipping off the heads of a couple of flowers and floating them on a shallow bowl filled with water.

When your guests are about to arrive and your table centrepiece is still unmade, there's no need to panic. Simply take the scissors to a couple of flowers and float them on a shallow bowl filled with water. If you also happen to have some floating candles on hand, the arrangement will be even more effective. For a long table, you could use several bowls, or even small individual bowls so you can give each guest their own arrangement.

A floating flower arrangement is also the ideal solution for broken flower stems that are too short for a conventional arrangement. Or recycle a bouquet, which is past its best but still contains a few flowers that are too good to throw away.

Choose dramatic flowers with large blooms such as lilies or gerbera. You could also use smaller flowers such as cornflowers, scattering several heads on the surface of the water. Snip off each flower close to the head, leaving a tiny length of stem to allow the bloom to take up water. Whichever flowers you use, perk them up with some cut-flower food, available from the florist, or add a teaspoonful of lemonade to the water. A light misting with a fine spray will keep your flowers fresh, too.

Fiery heads
A pair of gerbera heads in flame colours float side by side with gilded candles to make a sophisticated arrangement.

▶ **Oriental simplicity** *A dramatic scarlet amaryllis flower head looks wonderful in a small gilded bowl with matching glass pebbles. An arrangement like this would make a striking place setting decoration for a Japanese meal. A single amaryllis stem should provide enough blooms to make several individual floating bowls.*

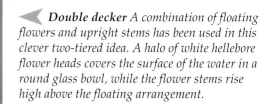

◀ **Double decker** *A combination of floating flowers and upright stems has been used in this clever two-tiered idea. A halo of white hellebore flower heads covers the surface of the water in a round glass bowl, while the flower stems rise high above the floating arrangement.*

▲ **Recycled bouquet** *Don't throw away a wilting bouquet; make a heads-only arrangement with the best flowers. In this interesting grouping, a trio of small bowls holds the heads of lilies and roses. When grouped together, and imaginatively combined with shells and pebbles, the flowers have renewed appeal.*

NATURE'S CANDLEHOLDERS

*Take your inspiration from nature to create candleholders with
a difference, and fill every room in your home with
the soft glow of candlelight.*

Don't keep candles exclusively for your dining table or living room. Try placing them throughout your home – in your hall where they greet visitors with a welcoming glow, or in your bedroom to create an air of mystery and romance; and what better way to let cares slip away than by relaxing in a warm bath surrounded by soft, soothing candlelight?

Candleholders made from natural materials are very quick and easy to make. You can use leaves, moss and flowers to create unusual and effective holders, or use shells from the beach for your inspiration. Wrap a candle in a leaf or place it in a shell, or float a tiny nightlight in a sea of flower petals.

Remember that lit candles are potentially dangerous. Ensure that the candle is stable and the holder is fireproof – never let a candle burn down to a holder made from plant materials. Avoid using conifer and dried foliage as they are highly flammable. If the holder is unlikely to contain all the dripping wax, do not put it on a valuable or easily damaged surface; alternatively, use non-drip candles.

▲ ***Bathroom bowl*** *A
shallow terracotta
saucer makes a perfect base
for a group of pillar
candles. Fill the saucer
almost to the top with sand
or gravel chippings, then
firmly insert the candles.
For a natural finishing
touch, add a layer of damp,
'teased out' moss.*

> **Marine theme** *Create a dramatically luminous effect with scallop shell candleholders. Glue a short candle on to a single shell, using a few drops of its own melted wax; or stick two shells together using a hot glue gun, to form open pairs, then place a tiny nightlight in each. To complete the seascape, glue a tall candle on to a smooth, sea-washed stone.*

> **Free-floating** *For instant elegance, combine a floating candle and chrysanthemum petals in a water-filled container. This lustrous chalice, with its raised bowl and light-reflecting finish, is ideal. If you are making a floating arrangement for a special occasion, always add the petals at the last possible moment.*

> **Sea shanty** *Add a collection of small shells to the base of a thick glass funnel candleholder for a simple seashore theme; pebbles or small, water-washed stones would be equally attractive.*

> **Leafy light** *Overlap supple evergreen leaves such as laurel or magnolia round a short, thick candle. Choose large oval leaves, wider than the candle's height. Lay the candle sideways across a leaf, so its upper edge protrudes slightly above the candle. Using a straightedge and sharp knife, cut off any excess leaf extending below the base. Secure with ribbon.*

CREATIVE NAPKIN RINGS

Add the final touches to a place setting with handmade napkin rings. They are quick and easy to make from odds and ends gathered from around your home.

Napkin rings are the perfect complement to a beautifully laid table, securing napkins in neat rolls, softly draped arrangements or fanfolds. You can assemble several napkin rings quickly, simply and inexpensively since they require very few materials. Search through your sewing box or remnant bag for oddments of braids, beads, shells and flowers – almost anything can be turned into an instant ring.

Match the ring to the pattern and style of your napkin fabric, or theme the whole table for a special party or occasion. They can be as simple as a twist of ribbon threaded with shells or an interestingly shaped biscuit cutter. Alternatively, in a few more minutes you can thread a string of sparkling beads or twist together stalks of silk flowers. Whatever you choose, it will bring the whole table to life, turning an everyday meal into a special occasion.

Circle of flowers Twist a single stalk of silk or parchment flowers with two or three flowerheads into a charming floral napkin ring. For an even circlet, curve the stalks around a cardboard tube, twist the ends together and cut off any excess. Bind with florists' tape for a smooth finish.

Braid rings
Ribbons and
furnishing trimmings, stiffened with
spray starch, make inexpensive and
imaginative napkin rings. Tone the ribbons
to match the napkins or opt for a rainbow effect, with different
colours on each napkin. Thread the ends of the trimming through
a large bead or simply tie them in a bow.

Adrift with shells Simple yet effective,
a length of narrow coloured ribbon is criss-
crossed and knotted around a triangular folded
napkin. Use a bradawl to make a small hole in a
shell, or use a pre-drilled shell – available from
specialist craft shops – and tie it on to the ribbon so
it rests centrally at the bottom corner of the napkin.

Clean cut Pastry and biscuit cutters come in
all shapes and sizes, from stars, crescents and
scalloped circles to animal and flower shapes. Perfect
for a themed celebration, they make unusual shiny
napkin holders; simply slip them over a folded
napkin and fan out the fabric folds on either side.

Little gems Cut a piece of picture
wire, about 50cm (20in) long, and
fold it in half. Thread a selection of
brightly coloured beads on to it, placing
small beads between large beads so the
wire isn't visible when you bend it into a
circle. Pull the cut ends of the wire
through the loop of wire at the opposite
end, drawing the beads at each end
together and forming a circle. Twist the
ends of the wire together and insert them
under the end beads.

PARTY TABLES

Add to the festive, fun-filled atmosphere of a special occasion
by dressing up the party table with sparkling fabrics, original decorations
and your most colourful accessories.

With a little imagination you can create a spectacular party table for any occasion whether it's a birthday, a family celebration or a themed party, a buffet or a seated meal.

Dressing up your party table need not be expensive – look round fabric departments for cheap and unusual materials to cover the table, and be lavish with quantities. A generous piece of shower curtain plastic, for instance, covered with a layer of coloured net produces a wonderful rainbow effect.

Break with tradition when arranging candles and use alternative holders such as coloured glass tumblers; or, for an outdoor party on a warm summer night, put nightlights in small glass jars and string them from trees – but be sure to keep them well away from the surrounding foliage.

▼ *Table hangings* Lay a pretty table or buffet – indoors or out – with a crisp, embroidered tablecloth complete with snowy white tassels. The tassels have been handstitched at intervals to emphasize the scalloped edge of the cloth. Drape the cloth so the tassels are shown to advantage round the table top.

▲ *Pretty in pink* On this romantic party table, metres of translucent shower curtain plastic have been shaped into a floor-length cloth then overlaid with misty tulle. The effect is pretty and feminine – perfect for an engagement party.

▼ *Garden glow* Put pink candles in glass jars and string them from the trees to twinkle prettily over a garden party table. Rose pink and ruby red accessories and fabrics continue the high summer theme. On a safety note, never leave lit candles unattended.

▲ *Alternative Christmas* As a refreshing change from traditional Christmas colours, try shades of melon, apricot and lime green, enriched with orange and gold. These colours look splendid with pine greens and shining baubles, creating a fresh and festive air. As a striking table centrepiece, fill a large glass goblet or vase with tiny kumquats and limes, and use it as a holder for bright orange candles.

PRESENTING GIFTS

The way you present a gift can have as much impact as the gift itself. Some presents are awkward to wrap, but don't worry, it's easy to make the gift really special by presenting it in an unusual way – you'll find lots of ideas here to start you off.

A watering can is almost impossible to wrap, so put away the wrapping paper and simply add some cheery flowers and a festive ribbon bow.

Whole hearted Say it all with flowers – turn a simple bouquet into a message from the heart. Slip the flowers into a colourful tote bag and add a lavish bow and some big red hearts.

There is a lot of truth to the saying that giving a present can be as rewarding as receiving one, but if you have ever tried to wrap up a watering can or a bottle of wine, you will know that some presents are not easily disguised. Typical gifts, such as a book or cassette, are easy to recognize too. The easiest solution to this problem is not to wrap them. You can often make more of an impact without swamping the present with a lot of wrapping paper – just let the gift speak for itself.

If you are going to stay with friends or you're off to a birthday party, for example, make a dramatic entrance. Arrive with a vase, tied with a bow, or wrapped in coloured, transparent cellophane, and filled with long-stemmed flowers. The vase will look striking, and can be put on display immediately.

Gift wrap usually gets thrown in the dustbin as soon as a present is opened. As an alternative, use plain, inexpensive paper, such as newspaper or brown paper, and add useful or decorative objects, such as sweets or other small gifts.

Sweets for my sweet Here's a great way to carry bottles to a party for a friend with a sweet tooth. Paint the bucket in a jolly colour and glue brightly wrapped hard candy round the edge.

Plain wrapping For a loved one with a garden, the ideal gift is a carefully chosen plant. Keep the wrapping simple, so it doesn't overwhelm the plant. Here, a box bush has been wrapped in plain brown paper and finished with a simple striped bow.

▼ **Paper money** *What better way to present a gift for a business man or woman? Wrap it in their favourite newspaper and then stick some chocolate money on to the outside.*

▼ **Wrapping with wellies** *Wellington boots can't be high on the list of gifts that are easy to wrap, so make the wellies the wrapping. Fill them with tissue paper and then pop some goodies on top – children will love them.*

Choose a wrapping theme to match the present that you have chosen. For example, if you are giving a large shell filled with soaps and bath pearls, finish it off with a natural sponge, rather than a ribbon rosette.

Functional gifts are expected at weddings and house warming parties, but many people are unsure about giving practical presents, such as kitchen utensils, for a birthday gift. In reality, most people are glad not to have to spend their own money on everyday items, so if you can think of a functional gift that a friend may need, all the better. Present a washing up bowl, gloves and hand cream attractively, and they will make a humorous and useful gift. It can be very rewarding seeing a present that you have given being put to good use, rather than politely gathering dust on a shelf.

Baskets are excellent for presenting gifts, and they allow you to give lots of small presents without having to wrap up each one individually. Decorate the basket with dried flowers and ribbons, and it can carry on its life as a household container: it can be filled with potpourri for the bathroom; used as an egg holder in the kitchen, or kept on a dressing table for storing cotton wool or cosmetics.

Frothy fun *Swathe a bottle of pink champagne with a length of pretty sheer fabric. Tie some glitzy gold braid or ribbon around the neck of the bottle to hold the fabric in place.*

Soap dish *A large shell makes a clever alternative to a gift basket. Fill it with small soaps, bath pearls and tiny natural sponges – it can be used afterwards as a soap dish.*

INDEX

Page numbers in italic refer to captions and illustrations

128

ACKNOWLEDGEMENTS

Photographs: 7-8 Eaglemoss/Graham Rae, 9 Eaglemoss/Simon Page-Ritchie, 10(tl) Houses and Interiors, (tr,b) Ariadne, Holland, 11 Plasti-Kote, 12(tl) Plasti-Kote, (tr) Hamerville/Home Flair, (b) Eaglemoss/Lizzie Orme, 13-14 Eaglemoss/Lizzie Orme, 15 Robert Harding Syndication/Homes and Ideas/Dominic Blackmore, 16(tl) Cowles Creative Publishing, (tr) Robert Harding Syndication/Homes and Gardens/Simon Upton, (c) San Marco Tiles, (bl) Hamerville/Home Flair, (br) Robert Harding Syndication/Homes and Ideas/Dominic Blackmore, 17 Elizabeth Whiting and Associates/David Giles, 18(tr,l) Rubber Stampede, (br) Hamerville/Home Flair, 19 Eaglemoss/Lizzie Orme, 20(t,bl) Eaglemoss/Lizzie Orme, (br) Cowles Creative Publishing, 21 Elizabeth Whiting and Associates, 22(t) Eaglemoss/Steve Tanner, (cl) Worldwide Syndication, (bc) Robert Harding Syndication/Homes and Gardens/Hugh Johnson, (br) Elizabeth Whiting and Associates/Di Lewis, 23 Robert Harding Syndication/IPC Magazines/Homes and Gardens, 24(t) Robert Harding Syndication/IPC Magazines/Homes and Gardens, (b) Worldwide Syndication, 25(t) PWA, (b) Elizabeth Whiting and Associates/Di Lewis, 26(tl) Elizabeth Whiting and Associates/Andreas von Einsedel, (tr) Robert Harding Syndication/IPC Magazines/Ideal Home, (b) Robert Harding Syndication/IPC Magazines/Homes and Gardens, 27(tr) Robert Harding Syndication/Homes and Gardens/John Suett, (b) Eaglemoss/Lizzie Orme, 28(t) Cowles Creative Publishing, (cl,br) Eaglemoss/Lizzie Orme, (bl) Elizabeth Whiting and Associates/Di Lewis, 29 Eaglemoss/Simon Page-Ritchie, 30(tl) Ariadne, Holland, (tr,b) Eaglemoss/Simon Page-Ritchie, 31 Robert Harding Syndication/IPC Magazines/Ideal Home, 32 Worldwide Syndication, 33(t) Robert Harding Syndication/IPC Magazines/Homes and Gardens (b) Worldwide Syndication, 34(t,bl) Worldwide Syndication, (br) Robert Harding Syndication/IPC Magazines/Ideal Home, 35(tr) Elizabeth Whiting and Associates/Jean-Paul Bonhommet, (bl) Robert Harding Syndication/Homes and Gardens/Chris Drake, 36(tl) Eaglemoss/Steve Tanner, (tr) Crown Paints, (c,bl) Elizabeth Whiting and Associates/Di Lewis, 37 Robert Harding Syndication/IPC Magazines/Ideal Home, 38(tl) Robert Harding Syndication/IPC Magazines/Ideal Home, (r) Eaglemoss/Lizzie Orme, 39 Robert Harding Syndication/IPC Magazines/Homes and Ideas, 40(tl) Swish, (tc,tr,c,cr,br) Ea/Sue Atkinson, (cl) Hallis Hudson, (bl) Artisan, (bc) Tenpus Set, 41 Robert Harding Syndication/Ideal Home/Di Lewis, 42(t) Elizabeth Whiting and Associates/Nick Carter, (b) Robert Harding Syndication/Ideal Home/Di Lewis, (br) Abode, 43 Harrison Drape, 44(t) Robert Harding Syndication/IPC Magazines/Homes and Gardens, (c) Worldwide Syndication, (b) Integra Products, 45 Robert Harding Syndication/Ideal Home/Simon Brown, 46(tl) Elizabeth Whiting and Associates/Andreas von Einsiedel, (tr) Robert Harding Syndication/Homes and Ideas/Dominic Blackmore, (cr) Robert Harding Syndication/Country Homes and Interiors/Polly Wreford, (b) Elizabeth Whiting and Associates/Gary Chowanetz, 47 Elizabeth Whiting and Associates/Brian Harrison, 48(tl,b) Eaglemoss/Lizzie Orme, (tr) Robert Harding Syndication/Homes and Gardens/Tom Leighton, 49 Robert Harding Syndication/Options/Jan Baldwin, 50(tl) Robert Harding Syndication/IPC Magazines/Ideal Home, (tr) Robert Harding Syndication/Woman & Home/Polly Wreford, (cr,b)

Eaglemoss/Lizzie Orme, 51-53 Eaglemoss/Patrice de Villiers, 54 Eaglemoss/Adrian Taylor, 55(t) Elizabeth Whiting and Associates/Di Lewis, (br) Marie Claire Idées/Chauvin/Chastres/Lancrenon, 56(tl) Marie Claire Idées/Chauvin/Chastres/Lancrenon, (tr) Marie Claire Idées/Gaillard/Chastres/Chombard, (cl) Elizabeth Whiting and Associates/Di Lewis, (br) Eaglemoss/Lizzie Orme, 57 Marie Claire Maison/Dugied, 58(tl) Marie Claire Idées/Marc Shwartz, (tr) Marie Claire Maison/Christophe Dugied, (c) Robert Harding Syndication/Homes and Gardens/Bill Reavell, (br) Eaglemoss/Graham Rae, 59(t) Robert Harding Syndication/Homes and Gardens/Trevor Richards, (b) Robert Harding Syndication/Homes and Gardens/Mary-Rose Lloyd, 60(tl) Eaglemoss/Graham Rae, (tr) Marie Claire Idées/Hussenot/Chabaneix, (bl) Robert Harding Syndication/Homes and Gardens/James Merrell, (br) Robert Harding Syndication/Ideal Home/Tim Imrie, 61 Ariadne, Holland, 62(tl) Robert Harding Syndication/Homes and Ideas/John Suett, (tr) Robert Harding Syndication/Homes and Ideas/Flavio Gallozzi, (bl) Eaglemoss/Graham Rae, (br) Robert Harding Syndication/Homes and Ideas/Ian Skelton, 63(l) Robert Harding Syndication/Homes and Gardens/Trevor Richards, (br) Robert Harding Syndication/Homes and Ideas/Dominic Blackmore, 64(t) Abode Interiors, (cl) Robert Harding Syndication/Homes and Ideas/John Suett, (br) Marie Claire Idées/Gaillard/Chastres, 65 Robert Harding Syndication/IPC Magazines/Homes and Gardens, 66(t,br) Robert Harding Syndication/IPC Magazines/Homes and Gardens, (bl) Elrose Products, 67 Robert Harding Syndication/Homes and Ideas/Flavio Gallozzi, 68(tr,bl) Cowles Creative Publishing, (cl,br) Eaglemoss/Lizzie Orme, 69(cr) Elizabeth Whiting and Associates/Di Lewis, (bl) Rubber Stampede, 70(tl) Marie Claire Idées/Chabaneix, (cr) Robert Harding Syndication/Ideal Home/Di Lewis, (bl) Marie Claire Idées/Chauvin, 71 Elizabeth Whiting and Associates/Andreas von Einsiedel, 72(t,bl) Robert Harding Syndication/IPC Magazines/Homes and Gardens, (br) Robert Harding Syndication/IPC Magazines/Country Homes and Interiors, 73(t) Robert Harding Syndication/IPC Magazines/Country Homes and Interiors, (cl) Elizabeth Whiting and Associates/Michael Dunne, (br) Ingrid Mason Picture Library/Mary-Louise Avery, 74(t) Elizabeth Whiting and Associates/Alfred Anghinelli, (b) Elizabeth Whiting and Associates/Alfred Anghinelli, (b) Elizabeth Whiting and Associates/Tom Leighton, 75 Robert Harding Syndication/Country Homes and Interiors/Andreas von Einsiedel, 76(tl) Elizabeth Whiting and Associates/David Lloyd, (tr) Elizabeth Whiting and Associates/Di Lewis, (cr) Robert Harding Syndication/Homes and Gardens/Bill Batton, (bl) Eaglemoss/Lizzie Orme, 77-78 Eaglemoss/Graham Rae, 79 Robert Harding Syndication/Homes and Gardens/Sara Taylor, 80(tl) Robert Harding Syndication/Homes and Gardens/David Barrett, (tr) Eaglemoss/Lizzie Orme, (cl) Elizabeth Whiting and Associates, (br) Eaglemoss/Steve Tanner, 81(tr) Elizabeth Whiting and Associates, (b) Robert Harding Syndication/Country Homes and Interiors/Alan Newnham, 82(tl) Robert Harding Syndication/IPC Magazines/Country Homes and Interiors, (tr) Marie Claire Idées/Christophe Dugied, (bl) Marie Claire Idées/Chabaneix/Chabaneix, (br) Robert Harding Syndication/Ideal Home/David Downie, 83 Cowles Creative Publishing, 84(tl) Robert Harding Syndication/John Miller, (bl) Cowles Creative Publishing, (br) Abode Interiors, 85(t,b) Ore

Designs, (cl) Robert Harding Syndication/Ideal Home/Lucinda Symons, 86(tl) Elizabeth Whiting and Associates/Nick Carter, (tr) Robert Harding Syndication/Homes and Ideas/Andrew Cameron, (c) Hallis Hudson, (b) The Pier, (br) Elizabeth Whiting and Associates/Nick Carter, 87 Eaglemoss/Graham Rae, 88(tl) Hamerville/Home Flair, (tr) Eaglemoss/Graham Rae, (cl) Robert Harding Syndication/Woman's Journal/James Merrell, (br) G.P.& J. Baker, 89 Elizabeth Whiting and Associates/Di Lewis, 90(t) Robert Harding Syndication/Ideal Home/Dominic Blackmore, (c) Robert Harding Syndication/Homes and Gardens/Pia Tryde, (cr) Elizabeth Whiting and Associates/Di Lewis, (bl) Robert Harding Syndication/Country Homes and Interiors/James Merrell, 91(t) Eaglemoss/Lizzie Orme, (b) Robert Harding Syndication/IPC Magazines/Woman & Home, 92(t) Elizabeth Whiting and Associates/Di Lewis, (cl) Ariadne, Holland, (cr) Robert Harding Syndication/IPC Magazines/Homes and Gardens, 93 Robert Harding Syndication/IPC Magazines/Homes and Gardens, 94(t) Elizabeth Whiting and Associates/Di Lewis, (b) Worldwide Syndication, 95 Elizabeth Whiting and Associates/Di Lewis, 96(tl) Ariadne, Holland, (tr) Elizabeth Whiting and Associates, 90(t) PWA, (tr) Eaglemoss/Steve Tanner, (bl) Artisan, 99 Elizabeth Whiting and Associates/Di Lewis, 100(t) Elizabeth Whiting and Associates/Di Lewis, (bl) Eaglemoss/Adrian Taylor, (c) Eaglemoss/Graham Rae, 101 Eaglemoss/Lizzie Orme, 102(tl) Elizabeth Whiting and Associates/Di Lewis, (tr) Worldwide Syndication, (cr) Elizabeth Whiting and Associates/Jean-Paul Bonhommet, (bl) Elizabeth Whiting and Associates/Andreas von Einsedel, 103 Eaglemoss/Lizzie Orme, 104(tl) Marie Claire Idées/Hussenot/Lancrenon, (tr) Elizabeth Whiting and Associates/Michael Dunne, (b) Eaglemoss/Lizzie Orme, (br) Robert Harding Syndication/Homes and Gardens/David Barrett, 105 Eaglemoss/Adrian Taylor, 106(tr) Ariadne, Holland, (c) Eaglemoss/Graham Rae, (b) Eaglemoss/Adrian Taylor, 107-108 Eaglemoss/Simon Page-Ritchie, 109 Eaglemoss/Patrice de Villiers, 110(t) Eaglemoss/Patrice de Villiers, (b) Eaglemoss/Simon Page-Ritchie, 111 Elizabeth Whiting and Associates/Di Lewis, 112(t) Elizabeth Whiting and Associates/Michael Dunne, (cl) Eaglemoss/John Suett, (cr) Marie Claire Idées/Giaume/de Lamotte, (b) Elizabeth Whiting and Associates/Spike Powell, 113-114 Eaglemoss/Adrian Taylor, 115 Robert Harding Syndication/Homes and Gardens/Jan Baldwin, 116(tl) Insight, London/Jack Townsend, (bl) Robert Harding Syndication/Woman & Home/Michelle Garrett, (br) Worldwide Syndication, 117 Eaglemoss/Lizzie Orme, 118(tl) Robert Harding Syndication/Homes and Gardens/Simon Brown, (tr) Marie Claire Idées/Dugied/Soulayrol, (bl) Robert Harding Syndication/Woman's Journal/James Merrell, (br) Robert Harding Syndication/Homes and Gardens/Tom Leighton, 119 Eaglemoss/Adrian Taylor, 120 Cowles Creative Publishing, 121 Ariadne, Holland, 122(tl) Elizabeth Whiting and Associates/Jean-Paul Bonhommet, (r) Robert Harding Syndication/Homes and Gardens/Simon Brown, (bl) Robert Harding Syndication/Homes and Gardens/Anna Hodgson, 123 Eaglemoss/Steve Tanner, 124(t) JahresZeiten Verlag/Wolfgang Kringer, (bl) Marie Claire Idées/Giaume/Lancrenon, (br) Ariadne, Holland, 125 Eaglemoss/Steve Tanner, 126(tl) Eaglemoss/Steve Tanner, (tr) Marie Claire Idées/Giaume/de Lamotte, (b) Eaglemoss/Steve Tanner.